YOUNG BROTHERS MASSACRE

T0170836

PAUL W. BARRETT AND MARY H. BARRETT

YOUNG BROTHERS
MASSACRE

UNIVERSITY OF MISSOURI PRESS
COLUMBIA and LONDON

TO DOROTHY

Library of Congress Cataloging-in-Publication Data
Barrett, Paul W.
    Young brothers massacre.

    1. Young, Jennings. 2. Young, Harry. 3. Homicide—Missouri—
Brookline—Case studies. 4. Police murders—Missouri—Brookline—
Case studies. I. Barrett, Mary H. II. Title.
HV6534.B76B37   1988   364.1'523'09778792   87-19156
ISBN 0-8262-0650-6 (alk. paper)

∞™ This paper meets the minimum requirements of the American
National Standard for Permanence of Paper for Printed Library
Materials, Z39.48, 1984.

PREFACE

On a bleak winter afternoon in the depths of the Great Depression, near the tranquil "Queen City of the Ozarks," Springfield, Missouri, one of the most bizarre events in the history of crime occurred. Ten poorly armed law enforcement officers and one police station buff, on the day after New Year's, 1932, set off lightheartedly in three cars to arrest two local farm boys for auto theft. When the carnage ended, after only a few minutes, six of the men had been slain, a record number of police officers killed in one incident in the history of the United States. That record stands to this day. This is the story of how it happened and of the unlikely people whose lives were changed forever.

The two mass killers came from the most improbable background imaginable. They were not products of an overcrowded city ghetto where street-gang rumbles were common. They were not victims of broken homes. Nor were they abused children whose moral upbringing had been neglected. They were basically farm boys from a peaceful tiny community, Brookline, in central Greene County, Missouri. The massacre itself took place at the quiet, orderly farm home of the J. D. Young family.

As recorded in a history of Christian County, Archibald Alexander Young, born in 1793, was the progenitor of the large Young family. He came to Missouri from Tennessee long before the Civil War and settled in what came to be known as the Nixa community.

The distaff side of the family, the Haguewoods, migrated from Virginia. These hardworking homesteaders were typical citizens of the Bible Belt, genuine fundamentalist Baptists to whom the idea of a "massacre" would have been unbelievable and abhorrent. The parents of the Young brothers, J. D. ("Daddy") Young and Willie Florence ("Mom") Haguewood Young, were, in fact, cousins. It was two of their sons, Jennings and Harry, who were to make history by killing the record number of police officers.

CONTENTS

The Young family. Back row, from left to right, Aunt Millie, J. D. (Daddy), Florence Willie (Mom), Lou Rettie (Rita), Mary Ellen, Mary Ellen's child, Jarrett Monroe, Oscar Ellis, James Paul, Major Jennings, Gladys, Willie Florence; front row, from left to right, Lyman Harry, Etta Lorena, Vinita, Mary Ellen's son.

Paul Young

Jennings Young

Harry Young

Owen Brown

Virgil Johnson

Frank Pike

Tony Oliver

Sid Meadows

Charles Houser

Wiley Mashburn

Marcell Hendrix

Ollie Crosswhite

1

HEARTBREAK FARMING
IN OKLAHOMA

For more than seventy years a formal photograph of the J. D. Young family has been preserved in the family archives. Frozen in the stiff poses typical of the days before fast photography, the father, mother, aunt, a married daughter's child, and all eleven children are lined up in order of age. Two dogs are included. The children are almost exactly two years apart in age. This photograph, taken in 1913, was made in front of the house that the Youngs built two miles east of Frederick in Tillman County, Oklahoma.

An earlier family album photograph, probably taken in 1908, was later printed in a history of Tillman County. This picture, too, shows James David and Willie Florence Young and their eleven children, each with his or her full name spelled out. Here the boys are decked out in hats, galluses, and imitation cowboy outfits. No one seeing these pictures of agrarian innocence could imagine that three of the sons would eventually establish long criminal records, much less that two of them would make history by killing the largest number of law enforcement officers in a single episode in the entire history of the United States.[1]

In the formal photographs the family members are proudly dressed in their best finery. In the earlier picture, Vinita is a baby in her mother's arms. In the other, she wears a knee-length white dress and long black stockings and is the only one sporting a white hat. Although one cannot see the color of her blue eyes, she is obviously a cherubic blonde. Beside her stands her sister Lorena in a lace-trimmed dress, black stockings, and high-laced shoes. A person looking at

1

such well-dressed naivete would find it impossible to imagine that the two sisters would one day ineptly trigger the
events that would end in the deaths not only of six police
officers but also, four days later, of the Young brothers, Jennings and Harry, in a hail of bullets in Houston, Texas.

The 1913 picture shows boys in peg-topped trousers, long
coats, and ties. Their hair is close-cropped and brushed.
Willie, the mother, in her black dress with high collar and tie,
typifies the dozens of overworked but proud women pictured in the ten-pound, handsomely bound history of
Tillman County. It took hardy women to follow the
explorers, trappers, trailmakers, and squatters westward.
Here, preserved forever in these photographs, are the homesteaders who settled and permanently established farm com-
munities in the course of the westward movement of
population.

In fact, the people in these portraits, dressed in their best,
are shown at the culmination of a colonizing process, not at
the beginning. The pictures do not give a glimpse of the
backbreaking hardships that were necessary to farm and to
build homes after the Kiowas and Comanches, the Plains
Indians of Oklahoma, were ousted from the land.

Tillman County had been a part of an Indian reservation of
4,639 square miles. In 1901 and 1906, the government
declared two openings for homesteaders for the grasslands
known as the Big Pasture. Adventurers and opportunists
poured in from all over the United States, Germany, and
Russia. In August 1901 alone, 200,000 registrants waited anx-
iously in Lawton for the land lottery. Among them was James
David Young. He came from Christian County, Missouri,
where he had been a farm renter.[2]

James (J. D.) Young filed a claim on 160 acres of farmland
two miles east of present-day Frederick. In 1902 he went back
to Ozark, Missouri, to gather up his family—his wife, Willie
Florence, and seven of the eight children living at that time
(one remained in Ozark)—and returned to Tillman County to

"prove up" his claim by what was rightly famed as "heart-break farming."

Like others, J. D. chartered a boxcar to make the trip. In one end were the Youngs' household goods, in the other their livestock. J. D., Jarrett, Oscar, and Paul occupied the middle section, while Willie and the other four children—Mary Ellen, William Jennings, Holly Gladys, and Florence Willie—rode, only slightly more comfortably, in a passenger train. (The remaining three Young children were born in later years.)

The journey ended for the train passengers in Lawton, a tent city. Three days later, J. D. and the boys arrived with their livestock and belongings. Together the family began a grueling two-day trip over all-but-impassable roads from Lawton to their campsite. On the first night, the pioneering Young homesteaders camped out beside the wagons, on Cache Creek. The next day camp was established on the bare 160 acres, and J. D. returned to Lawton for lumber.

Most homesteaders lived in tents or half-dugouts before breaking the sod and setting up even a one-room shack. Some lived in covered wagons while constructing a half-dugout. The Youngs built a two-room house in which the family lived for two years. A large cooking room was added later, and then a side room for washing and bathing. Not until 1911 would they construct the imposing two-story frame house of which they were so proud. They dug a cistern, and neighboring homesteaders camped out near the only drinking water. Two horses, a wagon, a one-row planter, a plow, a harrow, a disc, and a go-devil were standard farm equipment with which to make a living for nine people.[3]

The principal crops in the early 1900s, according to Oklahoma's Department of Agriculture, were corn, oats, wheat, hay, and some cotton. Even in the days of heartbreak farming, Tillman County produced 141,749 acres of wheat (17.4 bushels to the acre) and 113,391 acres of corn. Tillman County's per-acre value of farmland was among the highest in Oklahoma—$34.21 an acre. There were frequent droughts and other plagues.[4] One "heartbreak farm" daughter described "too few rains coming too late, hot winds blasting the wheat and corn tassels, hail that wiped out the crops and storms that wrecked the buildings."[5] All farms had gardens, plowed and harrowed by the men and tended by women and children. One year the wheat crop yield was 38 bushels to the acre. All farms raised their own hogs and chickens, and, of course, had two or more milk cows.

Although there is no way of knowing how much labor was required by each member of the Young family in "proving up" the 160-acre hard-scrabble land, it is a fair guess that everyone, regardless of inclination, worked hard. Every member of a homesteading farm family living on the land, in seasons of planting, cultivating, and harvesting, was compelled by circumstance to take some part. In the early 1900s all farm work—plowing, preparing the soil, planting, and harvesting—was done by horses or mules and hand labor. J. D., the father, was the dominant force of the family, and it is inconceivable that his healthy boys did not contribute to the labor force.

Jarrett stayed only long enough to help build the barn, and then he left home and Oklahoma forever, to an honorable and successful life. Oscar, Paul, and Jennings were left to help with the farm work, even though throughout their lives Paul and Jennings, at least, were notoriously opposed to physical labor. At best, a neighbor reported, they were "afternoon farmers." In the speech of the time and place, they were not "work brittle." Nevertheless, the official records of their prison careers sometimes list their occupations as "farmers." In their first detected burglaries, Jennings and Paul remained loyal enough to the homestead to ship their stolen merchandise to Frederick.

Of the homesteaders who failed, sold out, or abandoned their claims, there are few records. In off-seasons and droughts, J. D. walked into Frederick and did carpenter work on many buildings and houses, including the first red brick church. J. D., Willie, and Mary Ellen were charter members of the First Baptist Church.

Although Vinita was only four years old at the time, she remembers the family's moving from the four-room house into the large one. "Daddy bought the boys everything," she says, including bicycles. She remembers a "surrey with a fringe on top." At a county fair, "Mom" won a large "buggy blanket with a red rose in the center." Gladys, years later, remembered a "piano that sat in the parlor."[6]

Eventually, as Vinita recalls, "Daddy couldn't make it and we moved back to Missouri." J. D. was tired, she says, of eating out of tin cans because it was impossible to raise a garden or crops in the dry, sandy land. Even so, a knowledgeable and successful Frederick lawyer points out, in 1911 the farm was valued at $4,000 and on August 18, 1917, J. D. sold the 160 acres to Joel C. Barnes for $15,000. "So it would seem he made a good profit, finally."[7]

When the Youngs sold the Tillman County farm, they returned to Christian County, where they rented farmland. However, by March 1, 1918, they had bought that Finley River bottomland farm from L. P. and Missouri Gibson for $13,000, less than the sale price of the Oklahoma farm. Within four months, they transferred the title of this farm to John and Belle Canard for $13,500 and thus, ultimately, had an equity in the transaction.[8]

It was during this time that Paul and Jennings firmly established their careers in crime. It was charged in Christian County that on December 11, 14, and 15, 1918, they burglarized the Bingham Hardware, the Ozark Mercantile in Ozark, and, five miles away, the Efton Hawkins Hardware in Nixa. All stores were owned and operated by friends and neighbors of "the boys." Their father was so highly respected that he was accepted as their bondsman in all the cases without even the formality of putting up his property as security.[9]

Meanwhile, with proceeds from farm sales, J. D. and Willie Young were able to upgrade their place of residence.

On July 12, 1918, they bought a highly desirable 98.92-acre farm in Greene County from Ed R. and Maude Jackson for $13,000.[10] Although small in acres, this was an attractive piece of property in the community of Brookline, about five miles west of Springfield. One neighbor was the renowned Haseltine Orchards; another was the home of Lillard Hendrix. Hendrix was the brother of the sheriff of Greene County, who was fated to be the first person killed in the massacre of January 2, 1932.

The house was surrounded by eleven large soft maple trees and a few smaller saplings. Impressive as the trees may have seemed, they were to give inadequate protection during the massacre to Tony Oliver, chief of detectives, Sid Meadows, patrolman, and Charley Houser, the paddy-wagon driver.

At the rear of the house was an earth-domed cellar and, in the words of the wife of a later owner, "a cistern and little pitcher-pump."[11] It was from this vantage point that, during the massacre, Ollie Crosswhite protected the rear of the house only to be shot as he moved from the cellar's mound to the corner of the house.

A porch with four posts stretched across the front of the house, the ceiling just below the second floor. It was from in front of this porch that Virgil Johnson ineffectively fired a "gas gun" into an upstairs window. There were three bedrooms on the second floor, so located as to afford a clear view of the wooded lawn in all directions. The two-story frame house was painted white. It was from the rear door, off the kitchen, that Sheriff Hendrix was hit by a shotgun blast and Wiley Mashburn was mortally wounded. The red barn, down a lane from the house, closer to the road, was the refuge of several civilians and perhaps one or more police officers.[12]

The tillable land was fenced, and on the west side there was an old hedgerow. In the southeast corner was an unusual spring-fed pond, clean and blue. Vinita reported that J. D. stocked it with fish. One of her boyfriends, more than fifty years after the fact, remembers swimming in the pond and being served cookies and lemonade by "Mom."[13] Vinita was surprised to learn, recently, that the pond has been drained and has totally disappeared.

Today, in fact, the site of the "Young Brothers Massacre" is almost beyond recognition. Former owners Edgar and Priscilla Miller sold it in 1974. Now the old trees are gone, the house has been remodeled, all landmarks have been destroyed. More than fifty years later, the farm has gone full circle, returning to its pristine state.[14] Its appearance as it was in 1932 cannot be reconstructed. The scene is pastoral, peaceful, and quiet. It is impossible to imagine the carnage that took place there.

2

CRIMINAL CAREERS
COUNTRY STYLE

Their paths would cross repeatedly, and "Van" (William Luther Vandeventer) was a character worthy of notice in his own right. He stood out in any group for both his physical and his mental traits. He was tall and trim, almost totally bald. His face had a slightly Oriental cast. His sparkling brown eyes were alert at all times for an amusing aspect to any situation. Van was well known to the Young brothers in his official capacity.

Van was born in 1889 in the obscure village of Garrison in Christian County. He made the most of that heritage throughout his life by assuming with the unwary the role of unsophisticated hillbilly. In his youth he worked as a railway mail clerk, once a vital link in the nation's mail service. He attended the night Benton School of Law in St. Louis and later became nationally renowned in legal circles as a raconteur of Ozark tales of the law and courtroom anecdotes. He honed "Justice In The Rough," a humorous speech in the idiom of the Ozarks hillbilly, and delivered it many times, finally to American and English bars. The people and pieces that inspired him were "Comic History of the United States" by Bill Nye (founder of the *Laramie* [Wyoming] *Daily Boomerang* in 1881) and the English author Warren's classic satire, "Ten Thousand A Year," with its hero Tittlebat Titmouse and the law firm of Quirk, Gammon, and Snap.

Van was prosecuting attorney of Christian County from 1916 to 1918. He was the state representative from Christian County in 1920 and practiced law in Wright County with

Arthur M. Curtis. He was assistant attorney general of Missouri from 1924 to 1926 and first assistant and then United States district attorney from 1926 to 1934, the period in which the Young family encountered him as an adversary again. In 1944, after practicing law in Springfield for fourteen years, he became a judge on the Springfield Court of Appeals, a post he most competently graced until his death November 15, 1953.

While the rest of the Young family worked on the new farm in Greene County, Paul and Jennings firmly established their careers in crime, in country rather than city fashion.

It was only forty-six days after Armistice Day, marking the end of World War I. Patriotism still ran high. Most people thought that the Americans had primarily been responsible for winning "the war to end all wars." On December 27, 1918, the *Christian County Republican,* a weekly newspaper published in Ozark, ran a story praising the work of the local draft board.

The draft board may have been efficient, but even so, Paul and Jennings, who were of eligible draft ages (twenty-four and twenty-one), were exempted from service as "farm laborers." Their older brothers, Jarrett and Oscar, did serve, however, and were to be discharged at Camp Pike, Arkansas, in June and July 1919.

The *Republican,* along with testimonials for Foley's Honey and Tar Compound as a cure for "flu and grippe," carried an important proclamation by the editor, who also happened to be the mayor of Ozark.[1] This proclamation rescinded an order that had shut down public meetings, schools, and Sunday school and church services during the devastating influenza epidemic that would kill more than one-half million Americans. The war was over. The flu epidemic had subsided. Paul and Jennings escaped the epidemic as well as military service.

Ozark, population 798, was a typical rural county seat, dependent on farming. The town's sole industry was a cheese factory. Business buildings surrounded the courthouse square on all four sides, and alleys ran in back of the stores.

The automobile age was new. Only recently had the hitching posts around the square been abandoned. Citizens who were lucky enough to be able to buy the new-fangled machines could get them at local hardware stores. There were no garages in town; car owners had to depend on local handymen for repairs. Fred Estes and "Rooster" Forester (whose wife was a first cousin of the Youngs) were the town mechanics, the only fellows around who could fix a car. There were no paved highways, and highly inflated "casings" (tires) had a short life span, being quickly battered to bits by flint rocks and rutted red clay roads. The Young brothers took an early fancy to automobiles, even though they lacked visible means of support. This caused quite a bit of talk in town.

Ozark harbored no secrets; the town was too small for that. Gossip was the major local recreation. Paul and Jennings knew that people were talking about the fact that, although neither of them had a job, they were among the few people in town to drive a car.

Adults were critical and suspicious; but to the youth of Ozark the Young brothers seemed glamorous heroes. They carried with them an enchanting aura of sophistication. One boy, escaping the rain under an alcove on the town square on a chilly winter evening, found himself side by side with Jennings, who deigned to speak to him. It was an awesome experience. Many years later he could recall the false and haughty pride that would characterize Jennings throughout his life.

It was an established custom for Ozark boys to stay all night with their friends who lived on farms. On one such occasion the site was the locally famous Duncan farm, only two or three miles from Ozark. Some ten or twelve adolescent boys, including Bernice, Barney, Nick, Tommy, and Stooli Johnson, were guests of their friend Howard Duncan. It was late August. Crops had been harvested, and across the road from the farm home stood a large straw stack from the recent wheat harvest.

Before bedtime, in the twilight, the boys chose up sides and, around the straw stack, played cowboys and Indians. The Indians stripped to their waists, their chests and faces smeared with pokeberry juice. In lieu of Stetsons, the cowboys donned their straw hats. The weapons were sticks, staves, a toy pistol or two. Warfare was waged in and around the caves in the huge straw stack.

At sundown an early model automobile, a two-seated Ford without a top, drove into the field. In the car were Paul and Jennings Young, well known to all the younger boys as the only fellows in Ozark with access to an automobile. The Youngs had stopped to overawe and "goof the punks." They did not say where they had been or where they were going. The "punks" were duly impressed by the Youngs' opulence and sophistication and by the car. They noticed that there was a new battery-operated spotlight attached to the left side of the Ford and, in the back seat, some small tools and automobile accessories.

Gathered around the Ford, the cowboys and Indians were all silently but excitedly aware that some of the articles, particularly the spotlight, could not have come into the possession of the Youngs by purchase. Even the "punks" knew that Paul and Jennings could not have paid for these luxuries. Disturbed, and a bit fearful of accusation by association, the "troops," however, did not reveal their suspicions. They did not know that in some quarters the Young boys were even then under surveillance. Having made their nettlesome impression, the Youngs departed in a cloud of dust, and the "punks" resumed their game of cowboys and Indians. Finally exhausted, they spent the night soundly asleep in the straw stack.[2]

In any case, the Young brothers' activities soon became public. The first crime charged against them in Christian County was that on December 11, 14, and 15, 1918, they burglarized the Bingham Hardware Store and the Ozark Mercantile Company in Ozark and, five miles away, the Efton Hawkins Hardware in Nixa.[3] All three stores were owned and operated by friends and neighbors of the Youngs.

The December 27 *Christian County Republican* carried a story under the headline: "Robbers Captured." A subhead read: "Perpetrators of Various Robberies Run Down, Arrests Made and Confessions Obtained." The article was moderate in tone and far from sensational, even though in Ozark this was big news. Again, the reason for this surprising moderation was almost certainly the very high esteem in which J. D. Young was held locally. The report stated that an investigation "soon resulted in fixing the crimes on Paul and Jennings Young, sons of James Young an old and highly respected citizen of the county, now residing in Brookline, in Greene County."[4]

The official records of the case were restrained and precise and were written in the stodgy legalese of the day. The simple facts were, however, that the two brothers were accused of breaking into small-town stores in darkness and stealing merchandise. This may seem a common enough crime, but burglaries in Christian County were so rare that some store owners did not realize that they were victims until arrests had been made and some of the stolen goods were brought back. One "bolt of shirting goods" was recovered in Frederick, Oklahoma. Other loot was found in a haystack on the Young farm. Initially, there were three principal charges for offenses committed almost simultaneously, although Paul and Jennings had impartially burglarized almost every store on the courthouse square.

The first formal proceedings began with Van's filing a complaint for a state warrant in Justice of the Peace Court of D. F. Burgess, a full-time carpenter and builder by trade.

The records do not show whether Paul and Jennings were represented by lawyers or whether they were advised of their rights to remain silent and to obtain counsel. The doctrines of *Miranda* and *Gideon* were to come more than fifty years later. They waived preliminary hearings and were bound over on bonds of $800 to appear in the Circuit Court of Christian County at the January 1919 term. Their father, J. D. Young, was accepted as bondsman without even the formality of qualifying him as to financial worth.

It was charged that on December 14, 1918, Paul and Jennings had pillaged the Efton Hawkins Hardware in Nixa, a town where many of their uncles, aunts, and cousins lived. The local newspaper reported that Johnson Brothers' Jewelry Store had been burglarized, and "after an interval of several weeks other robberies in the same proximity came to light."

A second complaint charged that on December 14, 1918, Paul and Jennings burglarized the Bingham Hardware store on the west side of the square and again did "burglariously and feloniously take, steal and carry away four auto casings of the value of Eighty Dollars" and concluded with the inevitable magic phrase, "against the peace and dignity of the state." The witnesses, all formally subpoenaed, were D. W. Bingham, owner of the store; his faithful clerks, C. P. Cox and Floyd Hartley; and "Leck" Jones, all familiar to Paul and Jennings.

The third offense was the burglary of the Ozark Mercantile Company, specifically the theft of "one bolt of shirting goods of the value of Ten Dollars," which was found in Frederick, Oklahoma. We can only speculate what use the Young brothers might have made of such dry goods. H. V. Reid, owner of the Ozark Mercantile Company, had been the Youngs' neighbor. At the time, Paul was courting Reid's very attractive dry goods clerk, Jessie. Many years later one of Jessie's rejected suitors, perhaps too uncouth for Jessie's taste, reported dejectedly that she had said, "Paul is the only gentleman in town." Ultimately, however, Jessie did not accept any of the young blades but married her steady, reliable fellow store clerk. In time, they became the town's first successful undertakers.

It was no great feat and required no special criminal ingenuity to burglarize any place of business in Ozark in 1918.

There were only a few crimes of stealth—an occasional chicken-roost theft, a watermelon patch visited in the night—pranks not considered offenses worthy of the law's attention. The court's original docket usually listed crimes of personal violence, fighting, feuds, assaults, and an occasional murder. Homes were not consistently kept locked. Store doors were locked with only the simplest security devices. The storefronts were large show windows. The rear windows, opening onto alleys, were of simple design, and the locking devices were not adequate to frustrate burglars. The law enforcement officers consisted of a town marshal, a "night watch," the sheriff, and his one deputy.

The Young cases were not disposed of in January but were set for trial May 26, 1919. It is not known whether the Youngs employed lawyers, but on their trial date they filed affidavits for a change of venue and so must have had legal advice. They had been furnished the appropriate typed, legal form to know and solemnly assert that they could not have a fair and impartial trial "before the Honorable Fred Stewart on account of the bias and prejudice of said Fred Stewart, Judge against them." The allegations of bias and prejudice against Judge Stewart may have been a mere formality or a stall for time. Judge Stewart was a portly, florid man, smooth-shaven, and, though of course a law-and-order man, compassionate.

The Young brothers would doubtless have been fairly treated in Judge Stewart's courtroom. However, neighboring Judge C. H. Skinker "was called to try this case." Judge Skinker was a small, dark-complexioned man with dark brown eyes and a neatly trimmed mustache. He was the epitome of rectitude, fair but stern, with no understanding whatsoever of burglars. There must have been some negotiating (plea bargaining, as it is called today) between the prosecuting attorney, Vandeventer, and the Young brothers' lawyer, because the burglaries were not prosecuted to a conclusion. After whatever maneuvering took place, they entered separate pleas of guilty, on May 31, 1919, to grand larceny and burglary. Judge Skinker, the records recite, assessed the punishment that each "be confined in the penitentiary four years" for the larceny and "six years" for the burglaries.[5]

Their fingerprints and formal identifications were duly recorded by the Bureau of Identification at the Missouri Penitentiary. Their photographs, both side and front views, with prisoner numbers 21852 and 21853, still exist.[6] Paul was twenty-four and Jennings twenty-one "when received." The men were described as white males and their occupations recorded as farmers. Oddly, the records give identical weights of 125 and identical heights of 5'8 1/4". Their complexions are recorded as "sallow" (which may have been an editorial judgment), their eyes as "blue," builds "slender." The only difference noted in their appearance was that the color of Jennings's hair was "Med. chestnut," and Paul's was "Med. Lt. chestnut."[7]

Thirteen years later, after the Young brothers were nationally notorious, the *Springfield Leader*, in a specially boxed item, noted a special identifying feature of the brothers that perhaps adds a new and unusual dimension to the science of criminal identification. The headline read: "Young Eyebrows Odd Characteristics." The story went, in part: "Devotees of the art of criminology will be interested in noticing the photographs and descriptions of the Young brothers in at least one detail. All their eyebrows meet, the line of the brows is unbroken across the center—they look like twins in both front and side views."[8]

The penalties were imperfectly carried out. In their files, under the impressive seal of the state of Missouri, on large parchment-like sheets of paper, the "Honorable Arthur M. Hyde, Governor of Missouri for good and sufficient reasons appearing" and "for the purpose of parole," exercised his executive prerogative and commuted the sentences of "five years" from the date of sentence, in addition to the "benefit of the three-fourths law" (time off for good behavior). Thus, Paul and Jennings were tentatively released from the penitentiary for their first convicted crimes. Their country-style criminal careers were officially launched.[9]

3

YOUNGS ACCUSED OF
BOXCAR BURGLARY

On April 14, 1924, R. E. Truman, special agent, filed a complaint before the clerk of the federal court, the unyielding Tony Arnold, in his additional capacity as a United States commissioner. The complainant's solemn affidavit stated that Oscar Young, Harry Young, Jennings Young, and Mrs. J. D. Young, in violation of the Dyer Act, a 1913 act of Congress, had broken into a freight car moving in interstate commerce and had stolen a quantity of merchandise.[1]

This was the first time that Harry Young, then twenty years old, had been mentioned in criminal proceedings. It was also the first time that anyone had ever accused Oscar, who was later to become a respected farmer and a custodial officer at the United States Medical Center in Springfield. Furthermore, it was the first time that Willie was officially, and improbably, charged as an accomplice with her sons.

The accusation came as no surprise, however, to at least one person. Comer Owens, uncle and foster-father to baseball player Mickey Owens, was always willing to tell his view of his relatives, the Youngs, "as I heard it," or "as it was told to me." He told of visiting them and feeling with dire intuition, "I didn't like what I saw."[2]

Fortunately, J. D. had died in 1921 and so had to face only the humiliation of the first convictions of Paul and Jennings in Ozark.

R. E. Truman, who filed the complaint in 1924, was then a special agent (a security officer) for the St. Louis and San Francisco (Frisco) Railroad. Known as General Truman in later years, he was a first cousin of President Truman. An intimate of the Truman family, Colonel Rufus Burrus, said in 1984 that "he was more a brother than a cousin." He is represented in the Truman Library in Independence by a niche and his two-star general's flag.[3]

To his detractors and the irreverent, he was known as "Snapper" Truman, and he lived up to that image with gusto. Once an overexuberant guest leaving the lounge in the Colonial Hotel in Springfield announced loudly to some convivial companions that "Truman [the president] is a son-of-a-bitch." The unsuspecting stranger had the honor and distinction of being decked by a right fist to the jaw by a red-faced, enraged retired major general.[4] Reputedly, it was his personal challenge to violent protesting pickets that broke the railroad strike in 1923.

He was single-mindedly devoted to duty and law enforcement. On Truman's death, Senator Stuart Symington noted that he was "a veteran of four wars," beginning with his enlisting at age eighteen for the Spanish-American War. "He served with distinction in the Philippine Insurrection, the Mexican Border Wars and in World War I," said Symington.[5] The *Independence Examiner* reported that, in the Battle of the Argonne, "he received a battlefield promotion to Major."[6]

General Truman was a sturdy, square-shouldered man with a natural military manner. His hair was reddish-blond, and his glasses were always sparkling clean in typical Truman fashion. His hat was always precisely and squarely set on a perfectly tonsured head. General Truman hated cowardice and weakness of character. For petty thievery, in his book, the sole remedy should be extirpation.

It is not known what proof General Truman had to support his 1924 complaint against the Youngs. Some direct evidence must have connected Jennings, at least, with stolen merchandise; but if General Truman had more than mere suspicion to connect Oscar, Harry, and Mrs. Young with the offense, that cannot be documented. He may have heard the rumor, circulated by one visitor to the Young home, that when he "stepped in the living room, he was ankle-deep in carpets." This rumor falls into the class of hearsay observations, such as those given by Comer Owens. General Truman may have thought that joining and charging Oscar, Harry, and Mrs. Young even on slight evidence would force cooperation, perhaps even a confession, from Jennings.

On the basis of the complaint, the commissioner issued warrants charging all four accused Young family members with breaking the seal on a freight car and stealing specified merchandise. Bonds of $5,000 were fixed for Oscar, Harry, and Jennings to appear in court on October 1, 1924. Mrs. Young's bond was fixed at $1,000. This may cast some doubt on the good faith of all the charges. However, the judge might have thought that she would escape or not appear in court.

Mrs. Young's bond was signed by neighbors C. C. and Mary Conn and "a witness to mark" of Harry Johnson. The principal obligor on Mrs. Young's bond, however, was her daughter, Florence Young, to whom the 98.92-acre farm at Brookline had then been conveyed. The "witness to mark" was the noted lawyer Roscoe C. Patterson. Additional bondsmen for Oscar and Harry were Vernon B. Wilder, M. Roudebush, and E. and W. M. Wilder.[7]

These details become significant when we examine the contemporary record of the title to the farm. On January 29, 1924, before Willie transferred the title to Florence, a deed of trust (a mortgage) from Mrs. Young to a well-known lawyer, O. E. Gorman, as trustee for Roscoe C. Patterson, secured a note for $500. Whether this was only part of the distinguished lawyer's fee, or the entire fee, we do not know. On May 7, 1924, another mortgage named Clarence Davis and George W. Thurman as beneficiaries. It reads, "This note is given to secure the payees therein against loss by reason of their signing an appearance bond for the appearance of Jennings Young in the United States District Court at Springfield on the first Monday in October, 1924." This shows that for Jennings it was necessary to secure paid professional bondsmen. Willie, in order to secure her son's temporary release from jail, encumbered and jeopardized her farm.[8]

Earlier, Jennings had been charged in Christian County with burglarizing a hardware store in Billings and stealing guns. On a change of venue from Christian County, he was tried at Mount Vernon, defended by both Roscoe Patterson and Val Mason. That trial resulted in a hung jury. When he was arrested on the federal charge of burglarizing a boxcar, he was working as a boilermaker's helper at the Frisco Railroad and was living in a room on South Jefferson Street.

After the complaints, arrests, mortgages, and bonds, and after the appearance on the scene of Roscoe C. Patterson, the results seemed an anticlimax. On October 7, 1924, a federal grand jury, dispensing with all preliminaries, returned a three-count indictment against Jennings Young alone. Only one burglary was involved, but he was found guilty on three counts: that he "broke the seal" of a boxcar belonging to the Pennsylvania Railroad; that he "entered the freight car to commit larceny"; and that he "did steal, take and carry away" the property.

The boxcar was resting on a side track in the isolated village of Nichols Junction, now a part of Springfield. Its contents are interesting: "one five-gallon keg mixed pickles" from a wholesale house in Chicago to Claremore; "two rugs 9x12 and one small rug" from Sears Roebuck in Chicago to W. J. Strack in Chandler, Oklahoma; "one case of marshmallow candy" from Chicago to Walker Faust Company in Enid; and, finally, "one pail of cocoanut" from a wholesaler in Chicago to a dealer in Okmulgee. These are the items that Jennings and his mother and brothers were charged with stealing, but they are not specified in the indictment.[9]

Exactly what occurred when the case came up for hearing in October is not recorded. On December 13, 1924, however, a revealing order declared that Jennings "desires to have this case disposed of in Kansas City, Missouri, by entering a plea of guilty to the indictment returned against him." On the same day, appearing with counsel, Jennings was duly arraigned, and "for his plea says he is guilty as charged." Judge Albert Reeves fixed Jennings's punishment as

imprisonment in the United States Penitentiary at Leavenworth, Kansas, "for a period of three years from this date."
Fortunately for Jennings, the sentences were to run
concurrently.[10]

When the Youngs had needed a lawyer in the past, they
had been represented by the incomparable Valentine ("Val")
Mason. In their extremities, in 1932, they would again seek
his compassionate services. The attorney they chose to
defend them on the charge of boxcar burglary in 1924, however, was the renowned Roscoe C. Patterson.

Senator Patterson, as he came to be, was a handsome man,
stentorian in the courtroom and on the campaign trail. For
many years he served the Republican party, its candidates
and causes. When he was only twenty-seven, he served two
terms, from 1903 to 1907, as prosecuting attorney of Greene
County. In 1920 he became a one-term congressman from his
native Seventh Congressional District. In 1924 he was a pres-
idential elector. In 1925 he was named United States district
attorney, for a four-year term, by Calvin Coolidge. He
resigned that office in January 1929 and was succeeded by his
friend and the Young family's old nemesis, W. L. "Van"
Vandeventer.[11]

It was in 1928 that Patterson became United States Senator
from Missouri. He was immediately accepted by an elite inner
circle of tobacco-chewing, poker-playing, bourbon-drinking
lawmakers. Patterson left as a legislative monument to his
career the introduction and shepherding through Congress of
the federal interstate kidnapping ransom law of 1933, popu-
larly known as the Lindbergh Law. He was defeated for a second term by the then little-known Harry S Truman and, out of
hundreds of forgotten senators, has thus become assured of at
least a permanent footnote in history.

In 1924, when the Young family hired him to represent
them, he already enjoyed a very high reputation. One can
understand why the Youngs retained him, even though they
had to mortgage their home to pay him. The liberty of the
family was at stake; their backs were to the wall.

It is impossible, now, to know just what Senator Patterson did to keep most of the family out of prison. He may or may not have engaged in plea bargaining. He may or may not have had difficulty, foolish though it seems that anyone would seriously believe that "Mom" would "break into a boxcar." The records in the case are now hopelessly confused, many of them lost forever in the caverns of the gigantic Records Center in Kansas City. Some papers were lost in the transfer of the case from Springfield to Kansas City. Others are simply buried in mountains of old court documents.

The only person whom Patterson represented, as shown by the record, was Jennings. After General Truman's complaint, the arrest of the Young family members, and the setting of bonds, the cases were never prosecuted to a conclusion. No record exists of any pleas made or any disposition of the cases. All that is known is that the other three Youngs were not tried or convicted. They returned to their normal routines and homes.

Only Jennings was tried; he pleaded guilty and was sentenced by Judge Reeves to three years' imprisonment in the federal penitentiary. One may surmise that Senator Patterson's services to the Young family were priceless.

Another talented attorney who became involved with the Young family was Val Mason, who, with Patterson, had defended Jennings on the charge of stealing guns from the hardware store in Billings. He was to be of even greater service later to Willie and Florence, her daughter.

Before becoming a self-made and self-educated lawyer, Val had been a "baggage smasher" for the Railway Express Company and then a police judge in Springfield. That office had jurisdiction over violations of the city code and misdemeanors, and legal training was not required for the elective office.

Val, born on St. Valentine's day, was a stockily built man, always impeccably dressed, usually in a gray suit. He had a shock of beautiful, flowing white hair parted precisely in the middle, and a ruddy, smooth complexion. He took inordinate pride in his hair, and it was obvious that he groomed it carefully. He was a shrewd judge of character, a hard-drinking man, and an inveterate cigarette smoker. Although not formally educated, he made up for the lack with good sense and good judgment and was known as the wittiest lawyer at the Greene County bar. Woe be unto any young lawyer who tried to get cute with Val in the courtroom.

One of the legends of Val as a police judge involves his handling of the only black lawyer in the area, a large, rather pompous man named Campbell. When Campbell appeared in a police case, Val addressed the lawyer's client: "Had it not been for your distinguished lawyer and his great presentation, I would have given you six months in jail. But because of Mr. Campbell's great presentation, I will give you sixty days rather than six months."

Val represented many criminals and girlfriends of criminals in the Springfield area. He was noted among them all for his complete, compassionate understanding and for his fair treatment of his clients. It was said that if one needed to contact or locate a madam, street walker, or other wayward woman, it was necessary only to leave her name and a message with Val, and eventually she would show up.

His most important service to the Youngs came after the massacre, when he represented Willie, Lorena, and Vinita in their criminal charges, none of which ever came to trial. Then, in March 1932, a second-hand car dealer filed a suit against Willie and Florence and attached the farm, alleging the fraudulent sale of a stolen automobile. Val filed an answer and a plea in abatement of the attachment, denying all charges. In the end, the record recites that the dealer "will not further prosecute this cause" and "voluntarily dismissed the same" at his costs.[12] In the abstract of title to the Young farm in Brookline is a deed of trust with Val Mason as the beneficiary, securing a note to him in the sum of $1,000, his fee, of course. The note is for $1,000 even though the deed of trust secures a note in the sum of $2,500. In any event, by the time Willie sold the farm, this and all other obligations had been discharged.[13]

Val Mason's personal acquaintance with the prosecuting officials, Dan Nee and his assistants, Charles Chalender and Jim Hornbostel, on the county level and the United States district attorney, William Vandeventer, on the federal level was used by Val to good advantage to extricate Willie and her daughters from their predicaments.

4

PAUL ON A CAREER
PATH OF HIS OWN

One may wonder why Paul was not involved in the burglary of the boxcars. The explanation is simple. He had gone off on a lark of his own and was faced with monumental problems. He had, for the moment, moved his operations to Bell County, Texas. There, on January 14, 1924, the sheriff was directed to arrest him on an indictment charging him with burglary. Witnesses from the nearby towns of Temple, Pendleton, Belton, Franco, Waco, and Mart were subpoenaed to appear at the courthouse in Belton on January 18. There a grand jury charged that on December 10, 1923, in Bell County, Paul "did enter a house" owned and occupied by J. H. Ashcroft in which there was "corporeal personal property" that Paul appropriated to his own "use and benefit." Paul was represented by a lawyer, and the case proceeded to trial. It ended in an unusual manner.

A jury was selected. Judge Lewis H. James gave the jurors a written statement saying that the defendant was charged with burglary to which "he has 'pleaded guilty'"; and notwithstanding that "the court has admonished him of the consequences" and "it plainly appearing to the court that the defendant is sane" and not influenced by considerations "of fear, nor any persuasive or delusive hope of pardon," the court received the plea and instructed the jury "to find the defendant guilty as charged." Under the judge's instruction, the jury duly found Paul guilty and fixed his punishment at ten years in the Texas State Penitentiary at Huntsville.[1]

The Texas penitentiary records give a succinct "Description of Convict When Received." His age is listed as twenty-nine; eyes, blue; complexion, fair; weight, 130. Under "marks, scars and remarks" is the statement, "Last three toes off a right foot." In a newspaper interview after the massacre, Willie mentioned that Paul had shot off the toes himself, "accidentally" (to escape the draft in 1918). His occupation is listed as "salesman," which for want of a better designation may apply, somewhat humorously. His amount of education is given as fourteen years, including two years of college.

His wife's name is listed as Ludora Young, McGregor, Texas. Ludora must have dropped out of Paul's life soon after his conviction. Vinita believes that his wife in 1984 was his second and that he was divorced from his first wife. The Greene County records for January 1932 note that a Dortha Young, the "innocent and injured party," was granted a divorce from Paul. This was, of course, before the days of no-fault divorce.

One glimpse of Paul as a convict is provided by another part of the Texas penitentiary file, that of April 6, 1924. The page is headed "Convict's Biography." The account is as amusing for what is not said as for what is included. According to the report, doubtless provided by Paul, he did not drink, gamble, or use tobacco. From this information we are to infer, perhaps, that he was free from vice in any form, even though the record states that he did not belong to a church. (His Phillips University records show him declared "a Presbyterian.") Here, his occupation as "salesman" shows "seven years' experience." This was a gross exaggeration, if one considers only legitimate employment. When he was released from the Missouri penitentiary on April 11, 1922, he did work for the Keystone View Company. However, that was less than two years before his Texas incarceration. His family is listed as wife, mother, and two sisters: Gladys and Florence. Paul oddly overlooked his other sisters: Mary Ellen, Lorena, and Vinita. Two brothers, Jarrett and Oscar, are listed and their residences given; but he neglected to name brothers Jennings and Harry and to give their addresses. Opposite the query "Ever arrested before?" the answer given is "No," and opposite the question "Ever in Penitentiary, Reformatory or Workhouse?" the answer, again, is "No." Those answers, of course, are false.[2]

In spite of these early convictions, however, the rest of Paul's life was exemplary. Improbably, he was to become a respected, law-abiding nonagenarian, still alive in 1986, in a new home with a new wife. (He died in Houston, December 31, 1986.)

Despite the "no prior prison experience" attested to in the "biography," Paul, of course, spent almost three years in the Missouri penitentiary. There he must have learned how to get along in prison. At Huntsville, in Texas, he earned, at different times, 75, 78, and 81 hours of "overtime." By November 1924 he had accumulated 120 hours. Not only his good behavior, but also his very good luck, won his release from prison. In 1925, Miriam A. ("Ma") Ferguson was the governor of Texas. Her pardons of prisoners were so many and so generous that they made national news. Paul's signature to his "acceptance of the conditional pardon," witnessed by R. J. Ferguson ("Ma's" husband and former governor, if not governor in fact), was dated February 26, 1925.[3]

5

A BUSY YEAR
FOR HARRY

While Paul and Jennings were establishing their criminal careers, their younger brother Harry was not idle. Harry, whose full name was Lyman Harry ("Dutch") Young, began early to compile a record as lawbreaker that would end in his death, with Jennings, following their murder of six law officers and wounding of three others.

Harry's first offense of which there is an unimpeachable record was in 1925, when he was twenty-one years old. Upon a complaint of the prosecuting attorney of Greene County, he was charged with a rather new, and minor, offense: that he did "feloniously alter and deface the motor number on a certain motor vehicle, to wit, a Ford Speedster." That the offense was not deemed serious is demonstrated by the fact that the justice of the peace fixed bond at $1,000. The appearance bond was signed, of course, by "Mom," Mrs. J. D. Young. On November 25, 1925, Harry entered a plea of guilty and was fined $100, "which said defendant tenders here in open court." And so, on this, Harry's first offense, he was able "to go hence thereof without delay." Thus, modestly, Harry's criminal record began.[1]

It quickly mounted. In late 1926, he was arrested for buying stolen property. The property (household goods and furnishings, valued at $175) belonged to Glen Mason of Republic. Again, his bond for appearance in the Circuit Court of Greene County in November was signed by Willie Young and by F. S. and Emma O'Dell, Brookline neighbors. Compared to the feats of his brothers, this might seem a small crime, and it might have seemed to Harry to involve less personal risk than stealing or burglary; but it was, nevertheless, a felony.[2]

In what must have been an almost simultaneous event, an affidavit for a warrant and then an information in Circuit Court charged that on September 19, 1926, Harry did "steal and carry away one Ford Roadster automobile of the value of $400." The car belonged to Joe Cramer, a farmer near Republic. Three other witnesses—Jess Duvall, Tom Coleman, and Herschel Lawing, from Republic—were subpoenaed. The writ commanding their appearance in court on October 5, 1926, was served on all the witnesses by Ollie Crosswhite, later to be shot down in the massacre. In 1926 he was a deputy sheriff of Greene County.

The next event in Harry's criminal history was more serious. An affidavit for a warrant by the assistant prosecuting attorney, Gene Guthrie Deimer, charged that on September 26, 1926, Harry burglarized "the store of L. C. Shackelford" in Republic. It was charged that he did "steal, take and carry away one small safe of the value of $25, $325 in cash, and two pocket knives, an Elgin watch, fountain pen and a bracelet," all to the aggregate value of $380.75. This time the witnesses, in addition to Mr. Shackelford, were Ralph Wade, Alfred Owen, the sheriff, and, again, the ill-fated Ollie Crosswhite. A *subpoena decus tecum* (a command to appear in court, producing specified records) was issued to Matty Capron of the Grand Hotel, showing hotel registrants for the date of September 26, 1926. This writ was served by Ollie, this time a witness as well as deputy sheriff. Thus, the paths of Ollie and Harry crossed once more. The bondsmen, again, were Willie Young and the O'Dells.[3]

The fourth, and final, crime in this one-year series in Harry's life took place on February 6, 1927. Assistant prosecuting attorney Charles L. Chalender filed an affidavit before the "Municipal and ex officio Justice of the Peace" charging that Harry had burglarized the City Service Oil Company filling station, 998 Jefferson Street, Springfield, and did "steal, take and carry away $50.66 in checks and $75

in cash, good and lawful money of the United States." A preliminary hearing was waived, and this time, in default of a
$3,000 bond, Harry was committed to the Greene County
Jail. We may speculate that Willie was, at last, tired of making
bail for her son, or that she was unable to come up with so
much money. The witnesses called to appear in Circuit Court
on April 4, 1927, were the well-known Al Sampey, a portly,
quiet detective; Hank Teaff, a detective-lawyer; and Scott
Curtis, constable, who would play a large part in the after-
math of the Young brothers massacre five years later.

On March 28, 1927, all four of these cases were on the
docket of the Criminal Court of Greene County for final disposition. The name of Harry's attorney does not appear. Furthermore, there had been a change in prosecuting attorneys.
It was obvious, however, that negotiations had taken place
between Harry's counsel, whoever he was, and the state's
prosecutor, Willard W. Hamlin. Everyone involved was
eager to dispose of these several vexatious cases.

The first three were dealt with quickly. In each of these—
buying and receiving stolen goods, larceny of the Ford automobile, and the burglary and larceny of the store in
Republic—an ancient legalism expressed in Latin was used.
An entry was made of a *nolle prosequi*, used and defined to
this day as *in the court's judgment*. In short, the cases were
dismissed, and the defendant was discharged, upon recom-
mendation of the prosecuting attorney.

The fourth crime was handled differently. In the case of
burglary and larceny of the filling station, there was a *nolle
prosequi* as to burglary. However, Harry entered a plea of
guilty to the larceny. The court acted promptly, as had no
doubt been prearranged by plea bargaining, and fixed his
punishment as imprisonment in the penitentiary for "three
years from the 28th day of March 1927."[4]

Harry was then twenty-three years old, and the prison
record lists his occupation as "farmer." He was described as
"chunky," 143 pounds. There was "a scar on back of head"
and "a small scar below left lobe near chin." His hair was

"light chestnut" and his eyes "blue." In an emergency, his wife was to be notified—Mrs. Frances Young, 737 South Street, Springfield, Missouri.[5]

Rather dramatically, on the sheet carrying Harry's prison number, 31,358, there appears an initialed statement in neat penmanship. It is the final disposition of his prison file: "About January 2, 1932, the above named and his brother Jennings Young shot and killed the sheriff of Greene County, Mo., and five associate officers and escaped to Houston, Texas, where they were surrounded and captured on January 5, 1932, having committed suicide before they were taken." The author, apparently, failed to see the contradiction in his conclusion to this solemn pronouncement.

Harry was credited with "92 days merit time" and was discharged from the Missouri Penitentiary on September 26, 1928, one year, six months, and one day from a fully served sentence.

HARRY AND "PRETTY BOY" FLOYD

Rumor piled upon wild rumor at the time of the massacre. The most persistent was that Jennings and Harry were not the only gunmen involved. It was probably difficult for anyone to believe, or to admit, that only two untrained gunmen could create such devastation. The most popular candidate for the fellow-gunman position was the legendary Charles "Pretty Boy" Floyd. This was not true, but a peculiar basis exists for the rumor. Harry and "Pretty Boy" undoubtedly met in the Missouri penitentiary while they were both there in 1927/28.

"Pretty Boy" Floyd's first conviction was for a St. Louis robbery. For that, he was sentenced to five years in the Missouri penitentiary.[6] He was obviously not a model prisoner, for the record shows that he was disciplined twice, sixty days each time, once for "possessing dope" and once for "assaulting a guard." (Floyd knocked him down.) We don't know, but can only suppose, that Floyd and Harry knew one another in prison.[7] We do know that, later, Floyd was curious about the Young brothers massacre. In 1982 Harry's sister Vinita, irked at the inaccuracy of a fiftieth-anniversary story in the Springfield newspaper, said in conversation, "I wanted to call them up and tell them that it was not true that people other than 'the boys' were involved." She went on to say, "While Mother and I were living on South Street in Springfield [after the massacre] he [Floyd] came by to see us, stayed a few minutes, said he wanted to know what happened." On another occasion, she said that while she and her mother were still living on the Young farm, shortly after the massacre in 1932, Floyd had paid a visit there. "He probably just read about it and wanted to see the place," she said. Vinita vehemently insists, in the face of the persistent rumors, that only Harry and Jennings were at the Young home on January 2, 1932.[8]

In a letter to the FBI, written a few days before his death, "Pretty Boy" protested that he was not involved as a machine gunner in the Union Station massacre at Kansas City on June 17, 1933. On that day, in a misguided attempt to rescue unworthy convict Frank Nash, four officers, including an FBI agent, were slain. (This tied the second-place record for number of officers killed in a single episode.) Despite Floyd's disclaimer, the Supreme Court of Missouri, in affirming the death penalty of wild, half-crazy Adam Richetti, stated, "All three [Vern Miller, Floyd, and Richetti] were identified by eye witnesses."[9]

FBI agent Melvin Purvis, a legend himself, was finally the person to run Floyd down. The Missouri court pointed out that in the fatal encounter, the machine gun that Floyd fired until the handle broke was the same gun that had been repeatedly fired in the Kansas City massacre. A witness to that massacre described one of the gunmen as "heavy set, broad-shouldered, with a round face, wearing a Panama hat turned down all the way, shooting a gun with a vertical grip."

HARRY SLAYS
MARK S. NOE

Republic, a bedroom community adjacent to Springfield, Missouri, now has a population of 2,488. In 1929, however, only slightly more than eight hundred people lived in the town. It had been an idyllic, peaceful farm community completely lacking in crime and violence. On the warm, star-filled night of June 2, 1929, that tranquility was shattered completely.

Mark S. Noe, a highly respected descendant of one of the town's early settlers, was on duty that night, as usual. Although his full job title was "city marshal and night watchman," his official "marshal" services were seldom called upon. He was primarily the "night watch." Noe was one of the few persons in town known to own and carry a handgun.

On the night of June 2, Noe's peaceful rounds were disturbed when two young men roared down Main Street in a gray 1926 Ford coupe. As reported later in the *Republic Monitor*, they were "drinking and rather disorderly."[1]

One of the young men was a Republic citizen: Orval Lafollette, age twenty. The other was Harry Young, twenty-five. Harry was also living in Republic at that time, with a wife of whom nothing else is known (not Frances). As Noe was well aware, both men were ex-convicts.

Noe had seen them earlier in the evening and was keeping an eye on them in his role of night watchman. Now they got noisier and noisier as they tauntingly sped up and down Main Street, in full view of Noe. He made the judgment, in his capacity as marshal, that their conduct had passed the disorderly stage.

According to Lafollette's account of the affair, as quoted in the *Republic Monitor,* the two ex-convicts stopped their car in front of the Ryan Cafe. Lafollette got out, he said, and stood on the right side of the car while Harry remained inside, in the driver's seat. Noe ordered Lafollette to turn over his gun, and Orval handed Noe a .25 automatic pistol.

The accounts of what happened next differ in some details. Springfield newsmen, recapitulating the events almost three years later, produced this dialogue:

The marshal said, "You're drunk again!"

"Well, what about it?" Harry replied.

"I'll have to pinch you."

Harry said, "All right. Get in."

The contemporary report is probably nearer the truth than this one, even though it is based on Lafollette's somewhat dubious credibility. According to Lafollette's story in the *Monitor,* the marshal ordered him to get in the automobile with Young and told Harry to drive to the home of Judge Kerr, the local justice of the peace. Both Orval and the trusting marshal got in the car for the short trip. Harry drove an even shorter distance, perhaps as far as the Shover Drug Store, and then produced a gun.

One account has it that the gun was in the pocket of the car door. Another says that it was in Harry's lap. In any event, as the car proceeded down Main Street, Harry and Mark Noe "scuffled for possession of the gun," and, according to Lafollette, the gun went off. He did not know at the time whether either Harry or Noe had been struck by the bullet. Now the coupe careened farther down Main Street, with Lafollette in the middle between the marshal and Harry Young. A block farther along, in front of Dr. Beal's home, Harry stopped the car. There, Orval said, he "slid out from behind Mr. Noe who was standing up in the car." When he had walked a few steps away, "a second shot was fired in the car," and "as it [the car] proceeded north, he heard a third shot."

Lafollette hurried to the home of his brother-in-law. Townspeople, roused by the unprecedented sounds of gunfire, rushed out of their houses. Led by deputy sheriff Harve Snider, citizens spent the night fruitlessly searching for Noe.[2]

On Monday morning two men drove up a side road a half mile from the home of Lillard V. Hendrix, the brother of Marcell Hendrix, sheriff of Greene County. As the men drove along, they saw the body of Mark Noe in the roadside ditch, "his hat and lunch by his side." They rushed to the Hendrix home, where Lillard immediately called his brother Marcell to report the discovery.

The Greene County coroner at the time was a renowned pathologist and amateur ballistics expert, Dr. Murray C. Stone, whose services were later to be put to use extensively at the time of the massacre. Dr. Stone said, in scientific detail, that the autopsy showed that Mark Noe "had been shot three times, two of the bullets entered on the left side of the head, one just below the ear and one in the back of the head with the bullet lodging in the brain. Still another bullet had passed through the right arm entering half way between the elbow and shoulder and coming out at the elbow." This established beyond question that in the "scuffle" that Orval had described, all three shots that he heard, in an unequal struggle, had hit the marshal and had killed him.[3]

The original records have disappeared from the dank basement of the Greene County courthouse.[4] It is known, however, that the coroner's inquest was conducted by Dr. Stone, with the new and diligent prosecuting attorney George Skidmore. The recorded verdict of the coroner's jury was that "Mark S. Noe came to his death by gunshot wounds inflicted by Harry Young or Orval Lafollette." Noe was buried in the Evergreen Cemetery in Republic.[5] Listing one share of stock in Empire District Electric Company, valued at $100, his widow Bernice received from the Probate Court an "Order Refusing Letters of Administration" (because his estate was too small to be administered).[6]

From that day on, Harry Young was a fugitive from justice.

A reward of $675 for his capture was posted by the city of Republic, Greene County, and the state of Missouri.[7] Rumors placed Harry in cities and towns all over the country, most persistently in places where his respected brothers and sisters lived. Three Springfield law officers were sent to Tulsa, Wichita, and elsewhere. Pursuing Harry were Sheriff Marcell Hendrix; his deputy sheriff, Wiley Mashburn; and the popular chief of detectives, Tony Oliver. Two years and seven months later these law enforcement officers, with three of their comrades, would confront Harry Young in a fatal meeting.

A newspaper reporter found Willie Young at 211 Walnut Street in Springfield. She said that only the day before, Harry and another brother, with their wives, had visited the McCauley Cemetery near Ozark to decorate J. D.'s grave. She was so shaken by hearing that Harry was accused of murder that she suffered a "near breakdown." She said to the reporter, "I don't believe it. It all seems like a dream to me." While the reporter questioned Willie, Vinita came in. She said that she "had heard the rumor but paid no attention to it."

Two and a half years later, Willie, again being interviewed, said of Harry that, since Noe was killed, she had seen him only "two nights and a day last summer" and at a New Year's visit. She repeated Harry's version of the story of Noe's death: "He and one other boy were just driving through town, when Noe came up to their car and told them he was going to arrest them, that they were driving recklessly." She went on to say that Harry had told her, "The marshal started to get in their car, telling them to drive down the street, and when Harry told him to get his own car, the marshal hit him on the back of the head with the gun. Harry said the marshal's gun dropped on the floor of the back seat and that in the scuffle it went off and killed him." She didn't think Harry even had a gun. When she was told that the marshal was arresting Harry for drunkenness, she objected, "Harry never drank. None of my boys did. The girls don't smoke either."[8]

"Mom" was, as always, loyal to her children, no matter in what trouble they found themselves. Harry's wife, however, according to Vinita, left for Texas and never was heard from again.

Harry himself was not publicly heard from until January 2, 1932. Willie thought he had been living in Houston, "first working as a boilermaker and then driving a dairy truck." In Wichita, photographs of Harry were once identified by several persons as those of a man who "engaged in the trucking business for several months, leaving late last fall."[9]

Wherever Harry was, and whatever he may have been doing between June 1929 and January 1932, when his body was found in Houston, Texas, he was a fugitive.

7

JENNINGS IN
JAIL AGAIN

There was no nationwide manhunt for Harry after Mark Noe's slaying, although efforts to find him were made locally. The usual "criminal wanted" bulletins were posted. Alerts for citizens to be on the lookout were sent to towns and cities in Oklahoma and Texas. In Greene County, Missouri, Sheriff Hendrix, Ollie Crosswhite, and Wiley Mashburn were on the lookout for a sneak visit by Harry to Mom at Brookline. It was known generally that he liked to return to home base. Rumors were widespread that he was involved in, and perhaps even the leader of, an extensive car theft gang.

The experience of Harry's brother Jennings in March 1930 lent some credence to this theory. Jennings was in the Tarrant County jail in Fort Worth, Texas, indicted for violations of the Dyer Act, stealing and transporting automobiles in interstate commerce. The indictment was in three counts: (1) It alleged that on February, 24, 1930, in Lawton, Oklahoma (the largest town in the "Big Pasture," near Frederick), he stole a Ford Fordor Sedan "belonging to J. J. Allen." It charged that he transported that vehicle "from the City of Frederick in the state of Oklahoma to the city of Fort Worth in Texas." (2) The indictment charged that on February 15, in San Diego, California, he did "take, steal and carry away" a Ford Sport Coupe owned by Herbert K. Putnam, and this automobile he "did transport from the City of Frederick to Fort Worth, Texas." (3) The indictment also charged that on the same date he stole a second Ford Coupe from Herbert J. Putnam and "did barter, sell and dispose of said motor vehicle to one Charles L. Lillard in Tarrant County."[1]

A jury was impaneled. Jennings pleaded guilty and was again sentenced to two years' imprisonment in the federal penitentiary. He arrived in Leavenworth on April 17, 1930, and, after being transferred to "Federal Road Camp #4," was discharged on November 7, 1931.[2] In less than two months he and Harry would execute six officers of the law and wound three more at his mother's farm home in Brookline.

There is no hard evidence that Harry helped his brother steal these automobiles. It is, however, unlikely that Jennings was able to steal them all and transport them great distances by himself. The record does not say when and where Jennings violated the Dyer Act; but on the very day that Jennings pleaded guilty, another man in the Tarrant County jail also entered a plea of guilty in the same court and was sentenced to a term of "fourteen months at the United States Penitentiary at Leavenworth, Kansas."[3]

Although we do not know exactly how Paul, Harry, and Jennings, three small-town punks, adjusted to the shattering experience of prison life, we can infer a great deal from what we know about the prisons and the prison system of the time. At the very least, we can be certain from their subsequent careers in crime that no reform took place.

The Missouri penitentiary, nearly one hundred years old, held an average daily population of 2,288 convicts. It still stands today, ugly and forbidding, much as it was when Paul and Jennings spent their first prison terms of two years, eight months, and twenty-seven days there.

The four high stone walls are topped with guard towers at intervals. Those invincible-looking walls enclose an incredible maze of drab and depressing prison cells and buildings. The practice of contracting prison labor to private enterprise had failed, and prison labor in the 1930s and later was used by the state for profit. The major industries were pants manufacturing and the making of brooms and rope, as well as some farming, in addition to laundry and kitchen chores. Prison labor was on a task-system basis, with no rewards or bonuses. Rules were rigidly enforced.

It is true that punishment by being placed "in the rings" (suspended by the wrists) had been abolished. However, "flogging remained an acceptable discipline," and indispensable "industrial labor persisted as a central feature of life in MSP." Chronic "troublemakers," "recalcitrants," and "the most difficult of prisoners still wore [black and yellow] striped suits [and caps] and all inmates marched in lock step to and from meals and work; guards standing to the sides."[4]

At the time the Young brothers served their terms, and even as late as the 1940s, one particular ward in the Missouri penitentiary was especially unusual and much feared. This was a single room on the second floor of I-Hall, sixty or eighty feet by thirty feet, with bare brick walls on three sides, an entrance door on the west, and barred windows on the east. A raised platform at the south end near the door supported a large cane-bottom chair, a throne as it were, for the burly guard who presided over the room. The shiny hardwood floor was marked off by black lines. Painted on these lines at intervals the width of outstretched arms were black circles, the size of a man's feet. In this dreary, soul-stifling setting, punishment was doled out for any infraction of rules, including failure to produce the requisite number of pants required by the task system. The culprit stood with his feet in the circles, facing the bare brick walls, for a specified number of hours. If a prisoner fainted (as he was likely to do), his shoes were removed and placed in the circles while he was unceremoniously dragged to a wall and propped there. When he revived he was returned to the circles, there to stand with his arms at his sides, facing the bare gray wall again until his time was up.[5]

Among those men being punished during one guided tour was a handsome, engaging black man. When asked what rule the man had violated, the guard said, "Hell, I don't know; but every time I come in here, that son-of-a-bitch is on that line."[6]

There is no proof that either Paul or Jennings was punished

while in prison, but an entry in Jennings's prison record notes his "refusing to work." This was a drastic violation of rules, which could have been punished only by time on the line or in solitary confinement.[7]

8

SPRINGFIELD'S FINEST—
VICTIMS OF THE MASSACRE

Greene County, Missouri, and Springfield, the county seat, enjoyed passionately unbridled political warfare from 1928 until 1932. Not only were Republicans pitted against Democrats, but the major parties themselves were also split on trumped-up petty local issues as well as on problems of national concern.

Certainly in 1928 national issues were cast aside for more burning interests nearer home. A bitter, mudslinging campaign for the office of mayor of Springfield was being fought. On one side was a lawyer, Thomas H. Gideon, Republican.[1] Opposing him was Harry D. Durst, Democrat.

Gideon represented the "good ole boys," wearers of black felt hats—in other words, the "common folk." In opposition was Durst, who represented the elite, socially sophisticated business interests. Both candidates had impressive qualifications. Gideons had been prominent Taney County and Greene County politicians, lawyers, and judges for many years. Durst, too, was a well-known lawyer and a veteran of the Spanish-American war.

As the campaign progressed, it became increasingly bitter. All scandals, past and current, real and invented, were dragged out, to the delight of a titillated public. The bitterness and feuding did not stop even after the election. In June 1929 a petition was circulated to recall the mayor. Lawsuits were filed, charges and countercharges were hurled. The competing newspapers had a heyday. At last, Gideon was triumphant. One of his first acts as mayor was to appoint as

41

chief of police one of his most diligent supporters and fund-raisers, Ed Waddle.

In spite of his lack of qualifications for the post (he had been a neighborhood grocer before his appointment on July 22, 1922), Ed Waddle made a fairly competent chief of police. He was an affable, backslapping fellow.

Nepotism was an accepted perquisite of the office of chief of police, and Waddle took full advantage of that fact. His brother, Henry, was one of three officers "on the desk at headquarters." Sergeant Waddle, the chief's father, handled the desk at the northside station.

Ed Waddle had been a diligent campaigner in Gideon's heated race for mayor. Furthermore, he had raised a good deal of money to pay lawyers' fees and other expenses incurred by Gideon during the recall campaign. The rumor in town was that he had collected much of the money from the meager salaries of policemen, city firemen, and other persons under the mayor's jurisdiction. In fact, the organization and use of the police department had been one heated issue in the mayoral campaign and the attempted recall. Efforts were immediately begun to woo the public and especially the business community of Springfield.

Stephen W. McLaughlin, the dapper clerk of the police court, doubled as the public relations man for the police department, hence his service as writer, editor, and publisher of a post-massacre brochure, "Souvenir Review of Springfield Police Department." In that 1932 publication, he listed a force of twenty-nine patrolmen, seven detectives, a motorcycle squad of seven, four desk sergeants, and a chief of police, an assistant chief, one "identification expert" (Jim Hale, formerly circuit clerk of Christian County), a matron (the one woman), one process server, and one janitor.

McLaughlin actually prepared not one but two brochures, both of which he called "reviews" of the department. In both he emphasized how important it was for the police to be friendly and cooperative with Springfield citizens, especially businessmen, many of whom had opposed Gideon in the mayoral election.[2]

He described the "School of Instruction" where men "are taught and required to have full knowledge of rules and regulations of police matters, which is acquired by intensive and systematic training in the various branches of techniques, acquainting them with the laws and ordinances they are called upon to enforce. And an effort is being made to minimize the infraction of laws and suppress crime of every nature." In a further effort to impress readers with the high standards of police training in Springfield, McLaughlin said that after being appointed to the force, men "are thoroughly drilled and trained before passing to full Patrolmen."

Despite McLaughlin's propaganda, there is no evidence that any program existed to train police officers scientifically in making arrests, much less in self-preservation, prudence, or in the effective use of the weapons in their arsenal. Even more important, as it turned out in the Young brothers massacre, policemen received no training whatsoever in how to carry out a siege of a manned fortress or in the techniques of outwitting and cajoling entrenched gunmen to give themselves up without injury to anyone. In 1932 the Springfield police were simply not trained for the harrowing situation in which they ultimately found themselves, as most law officers would be today.

As only one example, Tony Oliver, chief of detectives, had joined the police department from the Frisco Railroad's "coach building department" on October 6, 1926, and, in McLaughlin's words, "had served as patrolman and traffic officer on practically every beat in the city and in two years made 1,352 arrests for crimes and misdemeanors ranging from drunkenness to murder." Oliver did, from time to time, issue advice to his seven subordinates, but even his extensive experience did not prepare him, or any of them, for the ultimately disastrous events ahead. Also, the thirty-three uniformed policemen (including Charley Houser, the

"paddy wagon" driver) were assigned specific duties by
Chief Waddle and by Sergeant Brumley, who directed the
traffic division. In truth, however, there was no required
basic program devoted to the scientific training of
policemen.

In 1930 there were six "officers of the Motorcycle Division,"
three of whom would eventually be involved in the Young
massacre. They were proud of their Harley-Davidson motor-
cycles and clearly welcomed every opportunity to display
their skills in directing traffic and leading parades and funerals. Frank Pike was one of the motorcycle officers in 1928. His
photograph in McLaughlin's "review" of the police department shows him decked out in gun, boots, belt, and full uniform, although his bow tie is a bit askew. By 1930 he had been
promoted to the rank of detective. In that role he is well
dressed in a dark suit, white shirt, and tie, a man obviously
proud of his profession. His father had been chief of police of
Eureka Springs, Arkansas, as well as of Springfield, Missouri. Pike finally played a prominent and controversial role
both before and after the Young massacre.

Another motorcycle officer involved with the massacre
was Tom Fielder. By 1930 he, too, was promoted to the rank of
detective. He was a small man, bright-eyed and sporting a
neatly trimmed mustache. In July 1970, twenty-eight years
after the event, like everyone even remotely involved with
the events of January 2, 1932, Fielder had explanations,
excuses, and opinions to offer. His tale was more interesting
than most. He said that talk about arresting Harry and Jennings Young for car theft began in the morning of January 2,
in both the sheriff's office and that of the city police. His
father-in-law, Henry Gardner, the desk sergeant, told Fielder
to change from uniform to plain clothes and to be prepared
to drive the paddy wagon to the arrests in Charley Houser's
place. The time was undecided because, Gardner said, Tony
Oliver wanted to make the arrests well after dark, while
Sheriff Hendrix insisted on immediate action. Ultimately,

the posse did neither but left in the late daylight hours. Fielder, however, missed the assignment altogether.

The day before, Fielder had failed to recognize Max Fitch, the popular Commercial Street doctor, and did not see the medical insignia on his automobile. Tommy "clocked him at 55 miles an hour." When the doctor identified himself, Tom "didn't even give him a ticket." In return, the grateful doctor promised that if Tom came to his office the next day, he would give him a pint of Four Roses (aged prescription whiskey in those Prohibition days). On January 2, Fielder told this story to his superior, and Tony Oliver promptly advised him "to not waste time, but go ahead and get the whiskey as we might need a good drink when we get back." Thus, Tommy Fielder missed the massacre. Later, he and three officers would meet the hearse at Halltown as it neared the Greene County line for the purpose of identifying the bodies of Harry and Jennings Young, so that, as he believed, the Houston police "could claim a reward."[3]

The office of sheriff in Greene County, Missouri, as well as in rural areas, was not fully defined in 1932. Most people, however, believed that a sheriff should still be a western frontiersman—a Wyatt Earp sort of lawman. Sheriff Marcell Hendrix and his deputies were well aware of public image, and they did their best to live up to expectations. As was true for the policemen, there were no training programs, and any professionalism the sheriff and his men had was gained by experience alone.

Marcell Hendrix came from a pioneer Greene County farm family. His father had been a farmer. His brothers, Lillard and Tom, lived on farms in the Brookline-Republic area, as Marcell did before he was elected sheriff in 1928 at the age of forty-one. They were all neighbors and friends of J. D. Young and his family.

In 1928 the Republicans enjoyed a Hoover landslide victory, and Marcell piled up one of the largest majority votes of all time for a county office. He was the quintessential farmer-sheriff. His campaign literature billed him as a family man, a successful farmer, highly respected among his neighbors. One photograph of Marcell was taken in winter, outdoors. He is wearing laced boots, a long, open overcoat showing a white shirt and tie, and the ever-present gray hat, tilted back. He is peering into the camera, hunched forward, and about to smile. A sizable "chaw" of tobacco bulges in his right cheek.[4]

Hendrix's deputy, Ernest Hodge, a long-time farmer friend, was the office administrator and bookkeeper. Frank Wiley held the undesirable and unrewarding post of jailer. Wiley Mashburn had recently been appointed "criminal deputy."

In those days the sheriff's residence adjoined the county jail. Despite its location, it was a comfortable home for Marcell, his wife, Maud, and their three children—Glenn, fifteen; Merl, thirteen; and Maxine, five. Had he lived to see them grown, Marcell would have been proud of all his children, but he would have been overjoyed by Glenn. Glenn became a motorcycle cop and, in 1948, was elected sheriff of Greene County. He was reelected to that expanding office an unprecedented four times, serving for sixteen years, and became a force in Republican politics before his untimely death on December 9, 1967.

Lucile Morris Upton, one of Springfield's most gifted and respected reporters, wrote in her column "Good Old Days" of "a day of tragedy for Springfield and Greene County" fifty years after the massacre:

My introduction to it came shortly before 3 P.M. when I was finishing Saturday chores at the courthouse for the News and Leader. As I made my final stroll around the second floor of the courthouse, I saw Marcell Hendrix and Deputy Wiley Mashburn come out of the prosecutor's office, each carrying a rifle. "We may have a story for you after a while," said the sheriff. "I'll call your office if we do." Sheriff Hendrix was a man of his word, so I returned to the newspaper office thinking little of whether there would be another story to type before I would finish the day. About 4 P.M. Managing Editor

George Olds yelled from the news desk, "Get over to the county jail as fast as you can; Frank Rhoades [police reporter] says that Sheriff Hendrix may have been killed." I couldn't believe it. Hadn't I seen him just a little more than an hour ago?

Lucile returned to the courthouse, and, she reported,

as I reached the old brick jail which adjoins the residence of the sheriff and saw the face of jailer Frank Wiley and heard heartbreaking screams from Mrs. Hendrix, I knew there was no doubt of the situation.[5]

Ollie Crosswhite and Wiley Mashburn worked for both the county sheriff's office and the city's police department. They also served, on occasion, as special agents for the railroad. Both men seemed made for roles as lawmen of the time, and they loved their work. Like many of their fellow professionals, they were drawn to the work by the thrills and hazards, their enjoyment of physical confrontation, and a sincere and compelling drive to pursue and capture criminals. In another day, they might have been "bounty hunters." In fact, on the memorable day of January 2, 1932, Ollie was not on the payroll of either the sheriff's office or the police department. He was present only as a volunteer.

Ollie was tall—six feet, four inches—with sloping shoulders hunched forward and large hips. His arms were so long that his hands seemed to hang to his knees, and he had huge ham hands. He always wore a light-colored Stetson, and his pearl-handled pistol was always visible, etched " + white,"[6] Ollie's secret way of marking all valuable possessions. In an early family photograph showing him and his wife with three of their six children, his smooth-shaven face appears almost wistful. He posed for the picture in white shirt, neat suit, and tie.

Ollie's brother, Raymond Crosswhite, interviewed in 1985, is retired from the security service with the United States Medical Center in Springfield. He is like Ollie in size, appearance, even in gestures. He said that after Ollie was killed, his widow, Ethel, had a hard time making ends meet. She sewed and baby-sat but at last happily married a retired railroad man.

Raymond tells how, on January 2, 1932, Ollie had cleaned up and just sat down to an early supper, specially fixed for him by Ethel, of his favorite food—ham hock, navy beans, and corn bread. Before Ollie had a chance to take a single mouthful, Tony Oliver appeared at his door and said they had to leave right away. Ollie, saying that he would be gone only a few minutes, told Ethel to keep the meal waiting for him.

Later, Raymond got Ollie's gun, etched with the "+ white," and presented it to the Ralph Foster Museum at the School of the Ozarks near Branson. One of Ollie's sons gave the museum his handcuffs. Ralph Foster paid $300 for Wiley's .45-caliber Smith & Wesson double-action revolver with buckhorn handle.[7]

Wiley Mashburn was a strong, stocky, square-shouldered man who wore his light-colored Stetson squarely pulled down to his ears. He was fair and blond with cold blue eyes. Among his friends he was known for an easygoing, cheerful disposition, but he was over-fond of rough physical contact to the extent of downright peculiarity. For example, in October 1971 Frank Pike well remembered Wiley's "punching" unsuspecting comrades. On one occasion, the chief had paired them up on patrol duty, with Frank driving. Wiley punched Frank's arm so often and so hard that it became quite sore. At last, Frank said, "I stopped, pulled him out of the car and beat the hell out of him, got back in, drove to the station, and reported it to the chief."[8]

Both Ollie and Wiley were often accused of challenging suspects and inducing them to resist. Comer Owens, who was distantly related to the Youngs, said that over the years, in detaining Harry and Jennings, the two had "abused them" and that because of this, both Young brothers had vowed "never to be taken alive."[9]

In 1929 it was a daily ritual for requests to be made and

reports taken by the assistant prosecuting attorney from various deputies and agents in the sheriff's office. On one beautiful June morning, the two friends appeared, Ollie looking glumly subdued and Wiley in high glee, as they waited their turn to speak. There were pink and red splotches on Ollie's face. His nose was skinned and his lower lip swollen. Wiley happily reported, to Ollie's discomfort and chagrin, what had happened the night before.

The two friends, Wiley reported, had pulled "six punks" from a boxcar on the Central Street switch track. All were from Brooklyn. One of the boys—a lean Italian, aged nineteen or twenty—moved too slowly, and Ollie slapped him on the side of the head with his open hand. The Brooklyn boy said, "You big son-of-a-bitch, if that's the way you want to play, take that gun off and I'll play with you." Ollie eagerly unstrapped his belt, handed his holstered gun to Wiley, and assumed a belligerent, flat-footed stance. With his open, giant-sized hand he swung at the boy's face. The boy, in the tip-toe stance of a fighter, ducked and delivered a solid right and left to Ollie's soft belly. Surprised, Ollie swung again, this time with a right-hand roundhouse blow aimed at the boy's head. The Brooklyn boy stepped aside and, with right and left jabs, stung Ollie's nose and cheek. Ollie now swung wildly, only now and then landing a glancing blow. The quick young man methodically outwitted and outpunched Ollie at every thrust. Unknowingly Ollie had got himself mixed up in an alley fight with a Golden Gloves champion. At last, exhausted and swollen-lipped, Ollie was satisfied to resume the role of law enforcement officer. It had come to seem to him that the county jail was the proper place for the six trespassers. Needless to add, there was no request for a complaint. To Ollie's relief, the six poverty-stricken boys from Brooklyn proceeded joyfully again, "riding the rods" to "Erewhon." Wiley was never happier than when he repeated this tale to the discomfiture of his lifelong friend.[10]

In one of the countless strange coincidences that cropped up in the massacre, the last photograph of Wiley Mashburn alive was taken on the very morning of the massacre. It shows him in character, as always. On the memorable Saturday morning, the sheriff's office made a raid on violators of liquor laws, including Claude White, in Ash Grove. The picture taken following that raid shows Claude White in the middle, with deputy sheriff Ernest Hodge on the right and Wiley on the left, wearing his overcoat and Stetson. During the extensive post-massacre newspaper coverage, the *Springfield Press* printed the photograph in one of its extra editions of January 5. The caption says, speaking of White, that "Mashburn had a fight [with him] when White purportedly made an attempt to obtain a weapon when arrested." Neither Wiley nor White looks the worse for the encounter, although White may have skinned his right cheek.[11]

Largely because of his twenty-five years of experience, during which he filled every rank in the police department, Tony Oliver was acknowledged to be the leading law enforcement man in Springfield in the 1920s and 1930s. He was a large man, clean-shaven, his clothes usually a bit wrinkled. He was quiet and fair in his behavior to his seven-man squad. The detective division was known as the "plain clothes" or "fly cop" bureau. If the occasion warranted, Tony could be stern. He had a reputation, sought by all lawmen of the day, of unflappable personal courage and great physical bravery.

Interestingly, in 1928 Tony had taken part in a siege that involved the intentional assassination of a policeman by an entrenched killer. It is true that on January 21, 1926, city detective Albert Franklin was fatally shot by Clinton Hollingsworth, a deranged man who barricaded himself in a house on Hovey Street. However, no city policeman or sheriff's officer was intentionally slain until June 8, 1928, when desk sergeant Gardner received a call that a man had "shot and mortally wounded two women" in a house at 907 College Street.

According to McLaughlin's account in his "review," Tony Oliver and F. M. DeArmand were assigned to capture the

murderer. During "the exchange of shots between the murderer and the officers, Detective DeArmand was killed
almost instantly." Dob Adams, the culprit, was finally captured, found guilty of "premeditated murder," and
executed.[12]

More than forty years later, Frank Pike, then retired,
recalled the event. He said that Dob Adams "came out and
was going to peacefully surrender to him" when Tony "hit
him in the head with his pistol and knocked him down."[13]

Whatever the truth in that case, much more is known
about the Young brothers massacre and Tony Oliver's part in
that disastrous event. He was not the leader, because in 1932
the Young farm was in the county, five miles west of Springfield and, hence, in the sheriff's turf. Sheriff Marcell Hendrix,
rather than city detective Oliver, was the leader, and it was up
to him to decide how best to deal with the embattled Young
brothers.

On the day of the massacre, Tony was going out the door of
the Market Street police headquarters, headed for the Young
farm, when a Mr. Duerr stopped him. Duerr was a life insurance agent who had come to collect a premium and complete
an application for a $2,000 life insurance policy. Tony said, "I
don't have time for that right now. We're going to get a couple of slick dudes; but I'll be back in a few minutes. You wait
right here." As it happened, it was Mr. Duerr who
assembled the photographs of the policemen involved in the
massacre and presented them to the police department,
where they are now displayed in the new headquarters
building.

All six victims of the massacre were courageous men, and
all the families deserve our compassion. Less is known, however, about Sid Meadows and Charley Houser than the others, and little can be learned this long after the event about
their surviving families. We do know that Albert Sydney
Meadows, always known as "Sid," was forty-seven years
old in 1932. He was a native of Chadwick in Christian County
and worked as a hard-scrabble farmer until he moved to

Springfield and went to work in the northside shops for the Frisco Railroad. For his part in the Gideon-Durst mayoral campaign, he was awarded a place on the Springfield police force, first as a uniformed patrolman. By 1932 he had risen to be a member of Tony Oliver's eight-man detective bureau, with no training whatsoever.[14]

Sid was a large man, recognized by his coworkers to be courageous and loyal to the department. He had only recently married Mrs. Lillie Wilhite, a Christian County widow. Meadows's brother and niece did not meet Lillie and her three children until the day of Sid's funeral. Fortunately for the new Mrs. Meadows, the enterprising life insurance agent, Duerr, of the Progressive Life Insurance Company of Rogers, Arkansas, had sold Sid a $1,000 policy. A neatly typed letter of appreciation is dated January 11, 1932, only nine days after the massacre. The second paragraph says, "The circumstances surrounding the death of my husband are well known, he being one of the officers who lost their lives at the hands of the Young brothers on January 2, 1932." Mrs. Meadows said, in conclusion, "The policy was issued only recently, and I realize more than ever the value of life insurance."[15]

An eerie sidelight to the event was erroneously attributed to a niece, Mrs. Leslie A. (Lucile) Thompson, in a newspaper story commemorating the fortieth anniversary of the massacre. Her father, William Alexander Meadows, and his brother Sid were enjoying a visit some two or three weeks before the massacre, it was reported. William said, "I had a strange dream last night. I dreamed that you were killed; that a bullet went right through the middle of your forehead." Lucile said, "Uncle Sid just grinned and said, 'I don't believe in dreams.'" When Lucile and her father went to the Fox Funeral Home, her father pointed to the round hole in the middle of Sid's forehead. "See where it went?" he said, "Exactly where I dreamed it." Mrs. Thompson, sixteen years old at the time, now emphatically denies the tale as reported in the newspaper.[16]

Houser's first name is variously spelled Charles, Charlie, and Charley in police reports and elsewhere. He was twenty-nine in 1932, having joined the city police force in 1930 as a motorcycle cop. A photograph of the squad shows Charley with his cap tilted far to the right and back on his head. He is, typically, smiling broadly.[17] In only two short years his good nature and charm had made him very popular with fellow officers and the public. He always laughed and joked and drove the paddy wagon with aplomb. In 1981 Lucile Morris Upton quoted a story from the Springfield newspaper of February 1, 1931, which shows Charley in characteristic style:

Charley Houser stopped his patrol wagon outside the Market Street police station this morning and yelled through the window at the desk sergeant: "Hey, Sarge," he shouted, "I've got a load of drunks. What'll I do with 'em?" Sergeant M. V. Crain stuck his head out the window, looked over the situation and observed thoughtfully, "Well, Charley, the jail is full of hold-up men—I guess you can put 'em in the basement."[18]

Steve McLaughlin summed up Charley's short life: "He was always hail-fellow-well-met." McLaughlin reports that on October 22, 1927, he married Augusta Sutton and "as a husband, he was faithful, devoted and always cheerful."[19]

9

CLOUDS OF
DISASTER GATHER

It is possible that even if J. D. had lived, the Young brothers would have come to the same tragic and bloody end. Without him, however, that end seems, in retrospect, inevitable. James David "Daddy" Young, the patriarch of the family, was its stabilizing force. It was he who kept discipline. It was he who made the important decisions. It was Daddy who decided that the family should move from Missouri to homestead in Oklahoma. It was he, again, who decided that they should return to Missouri to farm in Christian County. It was he who eventually, on July 12, 1918, bought for $13,000 the 98.92-acre farm near Brookline where the infamous massacre would ultimately take place. All the decisions were made by Daddy. If anyone disagreed with him, the fact was unreported and was certainly ignored.

J. D. was an ideal citizen—law-abiding and a tireless worker. He had the highest respect of all his neighbors. It was his hard work and prudence that made the farm a going enterprise. Even after he sold off 10 acres to his neighbors, the Haseltines, the remaining 88.92 acres constituted an average-sized farm in Greene County.

Unfortunately, this stabilizing force and wise decision-maker was lost to the Young family. On November 4, 1921, J. D. died at age fifty-eight. It was speculated by some people that his three errant sons, who already showed signs of their ultimate destiny, caused their father to die of a broken heart. He was buried at McCauley Cemetery, near Ozark.

Management of the farm fell, suddenly and terrifyingly, to Willie ("Mom"), along with the sole responsibility of caring for and making decisions for the family. The farm that became her responsibility was both a valuable asset and a heavy burden. For a lone woman to manage, it was a large order.

The farm lies north and south. The roadway leading to the house is from the east, Haseltine Road, and is unchanged to this day. Formerly there was a road from the north leading to the barn, but that entrance now has been obliterated. The red barn remains unchanged, but where the chicken house once was a garage now stands.

Fourteen large soft maple trees stood in the lawn and were to be important in the gory drama that would be acted out there. A barbed wire fence enclosed the yard. There was a hedge fence along the west boundary line. It is one and three-quarters of a mile from that fence to the road now known as "M," along which law officers would travel to their doom. A recent owner of the house says that he cut down the last soft maple tree, and that all the trees now there were planted by him.

The house is a two-story frame structure with a covered porch across the front, only three steps up. Three upstairs bedrooms offer an unobserved view from the windows in all directions. The east upstairs bedroom is directly above the kitchen, its window above the storm cellar that once existed at the rear of the house. The upstairs rooms remain unchanged, but a large room with a fireplace has been added to the east side, and a window and door on the first floor have been eliminated.[1] Today the farm and house are a valuable showplace worth more than $150,000.

We do not know how Willie managed to keep the farm going in the depths of the depression. We do know, however, that she was obsessed by the need to succeed. She desperately wanted to follow in J. D.'s footsteps and to see his hopes and dreams come true. The trouble was that J. D.'s physical strength and vast experience were missing. Trying as hard as she could, Willie barely managed to hold on for ten years. Then, at last, she was overwhelmed by a fate beyond her control.

Oscar, who lived on a nearby farm, did what he could to help; but he had his own family to support. Willie's other sons were a heartbreak, not a help. Paul was in a Texas penitentiary in 1924, Jennings in a Missouri penitentiary in 1928 and in a federal institution in 1930. Harry was in a Missouri penitentiary in 1927 and 1928. After he murdered Mark S. Noe on June 2, 1929, he became a hunted fugitive.

Vinita was the child whom Willie could lean on for help and companionship. When J. D. died, Vinita, then a girl of twelve, was the only child living at home. She was Mom's pride and joy, and, although she was young, she soon proved to be a real help. She quickly learned how to can fruit, make jelly, and even make lye soap. She kept these skills and practiced them even in old age living in a big city.

Vinita attended the nearby one-room country school known as Brick School. After the ninth grade she went to Springfield Senior High School (now Central High). Following the usual pattern for country girls, she lived in various homes as a "hired girl" during the week, for room and board and $1.25 a week. The home of this sort that she remembers with fondest memories was that of the James family. Her employers operated a successful music store. On weekends she went the six or seven miles home, and Mom always sent her back with fruit and home-baked cookies. She spent the weekends helping with the household chores and going on dates.

Today, Vinita is not bitter or resentful about her girlhood. She thoroughly enjoyed her high school days. Although she does not remember particular teachers or courses, she does remember some boys, especially Bennett, her first romantic love. Vinita graduated from high school in 1928.[2]

One revealing piece of information about Vinita's high school career turned up five days after the massacre. The house then was in shambles. Police officers and others, voyeuristically curious, had searched through the rubble, ransacked rooms, and turned drawers upside down. In the debris an enterprising reporter found a card dated

November 1927, signed by Cora B. Ott, the renowned high school dean and counselor to literally hundreds of girls for more than two generations. On the card Miss Ott "regretted the irregularity with which Vinita attended school."[3]

For more than forty years Adolph, now a retired garment manufacturer, has been Vinita's loyal and protective friend. Before departing for World War II he proposed marriage. Today, Vinita regretfully and ruefully reminisces, "I said, 'Hell, I'd be cheatin' on you before you got out of town.'"

After October 1929, a widow attempting to make a living off the land was doomed to defeat. Vinita took any work she could find to help her mother pay the bills, most memorably on an egg-drying assembly line, cracking and separating eggs. For Willie, in addition to the ever-present tragedy of three errant sons, there were the burdens of mortgages, interest, and taxes to pay. In spite of all troubles, however, Mom and Vinita did somehow manage to survive until the fateful day of January 2, 1932.

Although the family's devotion to Willie was legendary, holidays were only sporadically observed. Sometimes one son or a daughter would unexpectedly drop by for a visit, but not often. Of course, the "three boys," as they were always called in the family, were frequently in prison. Mom tried to explain this later in an interview by reporter Beth Campbell. "After their Daddy died, just seemed like they wouldn't stay at home. I guess they just got tired of farm life."[4] Also, the Great Depression lay on the land, and travel was a luxury. Harry was a fugitive, living under the assumed name of Claude Walker, even to his bride. (During her subsequent unwanted notoriety the press was to dub her "the thousand dollar baby in the five and ten cent store.") Harry, alias Claude Walker, worked as a milkman in the Magnolia Park area of Houston. It was there that a carpenter, Mr. Tomlinson, would later, fatefully, rent a room to Harry.[5]

If the family enjoyed holiday gatherings at Christmastime 1931, the fact was obliterated by the events of January 2, 1932.

Vinita and Mom were alone in the farm home. On Wednesday night, December 30, 1931, however, "shortly after eleven o'clock," Harry and Jennings "unexpectedly arrived," each driving a Ford automobile. Jennings had been released from Leavenworth on November 7, 1931. In the next half-hour Vinita's sister Lorena her husband Albert Conley, and their four-year-old daughter arrived from Houston. Albert had recently lost his job as an ambulance driver and hoped to find work in Springfield. Repeatedly they later declared that they would not have come had they known that Harry and Jennings were there. Albert knew that they had been in trouble, and he disapproved. In a police interview he said, "If I knew the boys were going up, I would have gone to Waco to see my mother and waited a few days until they cleared out." He had seen Harry only twice before—the first time two years before and, strangely enough, the day before they left Houston on the trip to Brookline.[6]

The actions of Young family members on Thursday and Friday were pieced together only, in the press jargon of the day, "after extensive grilling" by the police and prosecuting attorney. When photographs of Harry and Jennings were plastered on front pages across the nation, information began to pour in. On January 4 the *Springfield Press* published excellent photographs of Harry, Jennings, and Paul. On the front page stared a grim Willie, and on the front page of the *Leader* appeared the caption, "Here's the whole Young family"—the family assembled years before in Frederick.[7]

Recollections, anecdotes, and tips poured in, some reliable and accurate and some of most dubious foundation. Popular St. Louis Street barber John Conley was one whose memory was jogged. He "never thought more about the incident until pictures of Young were printed." He recognized Harry as the man who on Friday "stopped at the shop shortly after noon, pulled off a heavy sheepskin coat, and climbed into his chair. He was quite a talkative person," Conley recalled. He said that he had just arrived from Texas. He said he and another man started from Texas with two cars but one of them broke down and they left it behind. Conley said, "The man had about a week's growth of beard and needed a haircut." He "asked many questions about persons and events in Springfield, showing that he was acquainted here, but indicated that he had been away for some time."[8]

Many other reports were not so convincing. A Kansas City tire shop owner identified a picture of Harry as "one of three men [along with "Pretty Boy" Floyd] who came to his shop and asked to store a car there. A Parsons, Kansas, drug store owner identified pictures of Harry and Jennings. He said they "held up his store and 16 customers last November 23" and escaped in a coupe with $4,000. Jennings was then twenty days out of Leavenworth.[9]

A crucial accounting of the actions of the Young family on Thursday turned up five days after the massacre in a Springfield paper. The headline read: "Youngs tried to sell a stolen car in Aurora." The story went on to say that at ten o'clock in the morning, Mr. Baldwin was making a deal with a man he believed to be Jennings. The seller, he said, "didn't dicker long on the trade and offered to pay the difference between the used car and a new one in cash." He went on to say, "The trader said that he lived near Brookline and gave a number of references, but none of the references proved very satisfactory." The car dealer told Young that he would "have to come back with more references before the deal could go through." A man accompanying Jennings, who remained outside, "has been virtually identified as Harry Young," the newspaper reported. Despite his misgivings, Mr. Baldwin did not report the suspicious incident to local authorities.[10]

Having failed with Mr. Baldwin, Harry and Jennings now turned to their gullible sisters for help in disposing of the car. On instructions from her brother, Lorena appeared that afternoon at Clyde Medley's used car lot on McDaniel Street with a Ford sedan. Clyde Medley, the first successful second-hand car dealer in Springfield, was a shrewd businessman. Throughout his long life he has been reluctant to discuss his brief involvement with the Young family. Furthermore, his recollection of events of more than fifty years ago is not precisely accurate.[11] It is Lorena's contemporary account that supplies the details.

She and Vinita claimed that they did not know the Ford was a stolen automobile. In any case, when Lorena appeared at Medley's to try to sell the car, Jennings and Vinita waited down the street in Lorena's car. The Ford was registered to "J. P. Young," which could have meant either "James Paul" or "Jennings P." Clyde Medley said that Lorena could not sell an automobile not registered in her name. To overcome that objection, the Youngs went to the office of "a notary public on the North side" and had the title to the Ford transferred from "Paul" to "Lorena."

The next day, Friday, Lorena returned and Clyde Medley, probably stalling for time, then explained that he could not pay the asked-for $250 on that day "because it is New Year's Day." He suggested that she come back the next day.[12]

Then he called the police. He told the desk sergeant that he suspected the car was stolen and reported that Lorena would return on Saturday. The police set up surveillance across from Medley's business. Medley sums up the sequence of events in this way: "The girls drove a car to my place and offered it for sale. I put them off until the next day as everything did not check, and I notified the sheriff's department that they would be back the next morning. Two officers waited all morning until they returned [on Saturday, the second] and took them to the sheriff's office." On January 3, the next day, one headline proclaimed, "Sisters Effort to Sell 'Hot Car' caused Killing." Another announced, "Arrested on Warning of Car Dealer Here."[13]

It is peculiar that this city matter was reported to the county sheriff's office. Perhaps Clyde Medley's information tipped off police that Harry and Jennings were in town. In any case, the sheriff's office and police department did not immediately spring into action. The sheriff and his force staged a liquor raid in Ash Grove on Saturday morning, and it was only late Saturday morning that they first became involved with the Youngs.

Several days would pass before all movements of members of the Young family could be pieced together. It was apparently assumed by the Youngs that the sale of the Ford only awaited the coming of Saturday. Harry may or may not have had a haircut on Friday as reported by the Springfield barber.

Newspaper accounts of the massacre dealt with the guns that fatally fell into the hands of Harry and Jennings. This provides a rough sequence of the events at the Young home. "Several years ago," the report reads, "Oscar bought a Winchester automatic shotgun (U171572) from 'another man' and 'about four years ago' Jennings gave Oscar a Remington 25.20 caliber repeating rifle (A5739)." Through their serial numbers these guns were eventually traced from the manufacturer to a retailer in Springfield.[14]

Jennings and Harry wanted to use these guns of Oscar's. In December 1931, however, Jennings was estranged from Oscar and especially from Oscar's wife, who was one of the local Conn girls. Thus it was Harry who appeared on Friday night at Oscar's home less than a mile away. Oscar later told prosecuting attorney Dan M. Nee that "he wanted to borrow them to go hunting next day." Oscar "gave him guns and ammunition." The next morning, Saturday, at eleven o'clock, "the guns were standing in the corner of the downstairs living-dining room" of the family home.[15]

Harry and Jennings certainly knew how to use these guns, as they were to prove. However, their skills, though great, were quickly exaggerated into preposterous legend. The tales were broadcast second- and thirdhand, "as it was told to me," as Comer Owens put it. Wild rumors began even as angry crowds milled about the muddy yard of the Young farm after the event. Typical was the account in the *Springfield Press* three days after the massacre saying of Harry that, "in a number of turkey shoots in Greene and Christian counties," he showed his skill by "throwing marbles into the air and shooting them in two with a small caliber rifle and shooting walnuts from a tree at a distance of 30 yards."[16] But it was the opinion of pathologist Dr. Murray Stone, coroner, ex-officio sheriff, and ballistics buff, that Harry fired the shotgun and Jennings manned the automatic rifle.

Oscar and his wife came by Mom's on Saturday morning, and Jennings went upstairs to avoid meeting them. When they came again that afternoon about 2:30 for a few minutes, they saw only "the shotgun standing in the downstairs room." From his investigation, Dan Nee was of the opinion that "Jennings and Oscar do not get along, and haven't for a long time." The prosecutor assumed that when Jennings went upstairs this time, again to avoid his brother, he took the rifle (his gift to Oscar in other days) and was there when the posse arrived sometime after four o'clock.

10

THE MASSACRE

The day of the Young brothers massacre, Saturday, January 2, 1932, was gloomy, cold, and gray. The low temperature of 34 rose to a high of only 40.[1] Lorena and Vinita had decided to go back to Clyde Medley to sell him the stolen car. Before that, they deposited Mom, Albert, and Lorena's daughter, Natalie, in Springfield, leaving Harry and Jennings at the Young farm.

In mid-morning, Lorena and Vinita set out from the Young farm in the car in which Lorena and Albert had come from Houston. They took both Mom and Natalie to the Smith home, 620 Madison Street, where the family of Jennings's estranged wife, Bessie, lived. Lorena's daughter, a pretty child, had been the subject of a picture in a *Houston Chronicle* supplement, "Amid Blossoms." The sisters dropped Albert in the business district to get a haircut. He was to meet them, later, at the Smith home. Lorena, Vinita, Mrs. Smith, and Mom ate lunch, and Mom went grocery shopping, agreeing to meet the girls downtown in the afternoon.

It was just before 2:30 when Lorena and Vinita arrived back at the farm to pick up the stolen car that they had tried to dispose of earlier and take it back to Springfield to sell to Medley.

Lorena and Vinita always insisted that when they left the Young farm that last time, only Harry and Jennings were there. Even more than fifty years later, Vinita still emphatically insists that "only the boys" were in the house when they left just before three o'clock that bleak January afternoon,[2] a fact much debated later.

Vinita and Lorena drove directly to the Medley agency

with the stolen car. They expected only to deliver the Ford with no further delay and to pick up the check for $250, Medley having already put them off twice.

The policemen, who had been parked across the street since early morning, spotted the girls immediately. City detectives Virgil Johnson and Lee Jones arrested the two sisters and took them to the aged city jail behind police headquarters on Market Street. The *Sunday News* later headlined, "Two Girls Held for Auto Theft Tipped Sheriff."

At first Vinita and Lorena denied that Harry and Jennings were anywhere near Springfield. However, as reported in the *St. Louis Post-Dispatch* on Monday, "after several hours questioning . . . the sisters of the fugitives changed their stories and admitted two of their brothers were at the Young homestead."[3]

From the start, the press exploited every possible angle of the Young story. A *Daily News* photographer posed Lorena and Vinita sitting cross-legged on a jail chair "where they had been grilled regarding every detail leading up to the slaughter." The reporter observed that on Sunday, the day after the massacre, Lorena wore "a purple silk dress with costume jewelry. Her auburn hair was pulled back tight to a knot on the back of her head." Another reporter described "slender, petite-faced Lorena." He could have added, as indeed another story did, that Lorena's chief concern and anxiety was for her daughter Natalie.

Vinita was "dressed in a black sport suit with tan shirtwaist and a black beret." Another writer reported: "Vinita, her short blond straight hair giving her face a hoydenish look was more sprightly than her sister."[4]

While Vinita and Lorena were being arrested and questioned, Mom had finished her grocery shopping and was waiting for them downtown, as it had been agreed. When they didn't show up, she went back to the Smith home alone. There she spent the night, distraught and worried about her daughters.

Under questioning, Lorena and Vinita admitted where

Willie could be found. Officer Jim Hale was dispatched to the Smith home to arrest her. Prosecuting attorney Dan Nee had her held incommunicado in the Greene County jail. The *Springfield Leader* reported the next day, "The bandits' mother, past 60 years old [she was, in fact, 65] was sobbing hysterically and almost exhausted from excitement and grief when officers found her." By that time she had become frantic about her missing daughters.[5]

Mom was described by a newspaper reporter as a "gray-haired little woman." Her eyes, it was said, were blue. Vinita later described her mother's eyes as "dark blue, very blue."[6]

In a very short time, Willie came to be seen by the press, the policemen, and newspaper readers eager for every detail as the quintessential grandmother.

By this time it was three o'clock on Saturday afternoon. From this point on, the details have become clouded by the enormity of the disaster and the speed of events. Police chief Ed Waddle felt that he could not send his men alone to arrest the Young brothers, but that he had to include the sheriff's office as a matter of protocol and professional deference. Although the attempt to sell the hot automobile was a city matter and hence in the jurisdiction of the city police, Harry was a fugitive (because he had been charged with Noe's murder) whose crime had been committed in Republic. Waddle felt that "they live in the Sheriff's territory and he would resent lack of cooperation." Thus it was that the sheriff was called and told that the Young brothers were to be found at the family farm.[7]

In a matter of minutes, Sheriff Marcell Hendrix arrived at the police station on Market Street, with his deputy sheriff Wiley Mashburn and special deputy Ollie Crosswhite. Detective Virgil Johnson jumped into the car with them. Senior officer Tony Oliver, along with Sid Meadows and Ben Bilyeu, took off in a police car driven by Charley Houser. Just as the two cars were on their way, Frank Pike and Owen Brown drove up. Pike, feeling left out of the action, complained to Chief Waddle, "What are they trying to do, put on a private raid? Why didn't they let us go?" The chief said, "You can still go, if you haven't anything else to do." A civilian, B. G. Wegman, hopped in with Pike and Brown to go along "for the ride." Wegman would ultimately prove to be a mystery man, unaccounted for in the denouement of the disaster.[8]

One person who might have gone along with the others to the Young farm on that day but who did not was detective Lee Jones. He was one of the men who had earlier arrested Vinita and Lorena. The newspapers made a special story of the fact that had he not been a barber before joining the police force, he probably would have been shot down with the rest. On the day of the massacre, Saturday, January 2, police chief Ed Waddle sent Jones to the hospital to shave motorcycle officer Oscar Lowe, a patient there. Thus it was that Jones was not at the station when the hastily assembled posse drove off.[9]

The police and the sheriff's men didn't bother to consult on tactics or stratagem at any time. There was no preplanned agreement on how to proceed. In fact, no one took the expedition very seriously. It was obvious that such a large posse—ten officers and one layman—was excessive. After all, they were only going after two small-time car thieves. It was only a lighthearted lark that would end in a routine arrest. The three carsful of men might as well have been boys playing cops and robbers. Everyone looked forward to seeing the two punks brought in, cornered and cringing. No one had the smallest suspicion that the criminals would resist being taken. The posse, it was supposed, would surprise the Young brothers and surround the house. The two-bit criminals would, of course, automatically surrender.

The only arms the officers carried were pistols and two tear gas shells. There were no rifles or shotguns. (The press, over-dramatically, called the shells gas guns.) Harry's record of violence was well known, but not one of the pursuers, in his wildest dreams, expected a shoot-out. Unfortunately, no one knew just how desperate Harry was and how little he thought he had to lose, having been a fugitive for two years on a murder charge.

The distance on gravel and macadam road from the police station on Market Street to the Young farm on Haseltine Road was six miles. The first to arrive was the police car driven by Houser, who parked at the northeast corner of the farm. The men held a short discussion of surrounding the house to keep the Young brothers from escaping. Tony Oliver and the others in that automobile—Sid Meadows and Ben Bilyeu, in addition to Houser— got out and walked across a field, through the orchard, and past the barn to the front of the house. No one looked into the barn at this point, so no one noticed the two automobiles parked there.

The second police car, with Pike, Brown, and Wegman, and the sheriff's car, with Hendrix, Mashburn, Crosswhite, and detective Virgil Johnson, drove up the north lane into the yard and parked side by side, facing the front of the house.[10]

The men got out of their cars and looked around at the quiet scene. There was no one in sight. It was now four o'clock. The only sound was the winter wind in the trees. It began to look as if no one was there. The only reason the officers had to believe that Harry and Jennings were on hand was what Tony had gathered from his interview with Lorena and Vinita. Neither Oscar, his wife, Lorena's husband, Albert, nor Willie had been questioned yet.

The officers surrounded the house. Still no one appeared. Still there was no sound from inside the house, no sign of life. Sid Meadows, Virgil Johnson, and Ben Bilyeu stepped up on the wooden front porch and knocked on the door. One of them yelled, "Hello, Jennings, hello Harry." Another shouted, "Oh, Paul," just in case there were three Young brothers inside. There was no answering sound.

Ollie Crosswhite and Charley Houser went around the house to the north side. At the kitchen door they, too, knocked and yelled. Getting no answer, they joined the others at the front of the house. Ollie pressed his face to first one window pane, then another, peering into the apparently empty front rooms. "By golly," he said, turning back to the others, "there's nobody in this part of the house. That's a cinch." He swore, though, that he heard someone walking somewhere inside. He couldn't say whether it was a man or a woman.[11]

"Let's unlock a door," someone suggested. Charley Houser produced a skeleton key and put it in the keyhole. No luck. The door was locked with "a key in the other side."[12]

Sheriff Hendrix was getting impatient. "Well, hell," he said, "I don't like to go back without finding out for sure whether or not those fellows are here."

At this point, the law officers, never well organized, began to behave impetuously and gave up any advantage they might have enjoyed. Unknowingly, they had given the Young brothers, surrounded and outnumbered, the upper hand.

Someone said, "If they're not going to open up and come out, I guess we'll have to kick in a door." Sheriff Hendrix said that he would take responsibility for any damage done to the house. He announced, "Wiley and I will smash in the back door."

Someone suggested that first a tear gas canister should be fired into the house. Virgil Johnson went to the police car and came back with one of the two gas shells. Since there seemed to be no one downstairs, Virgil hurled the tear gas shell at a front second-story window. It hit the window frame and bounced off, breaking the glass.

Now Sheriff Hendrix and Wiley Mashburn, followed by Frank Pike, proceeded to the back door. Almost certainly, the sheriff alone kicked in the back door, although at the coroner's inquest Frank was to testify that "three of us lammed up against the back door and it flew open."[13]

Immediately a shotgun blast exploded. The deadly shot blasted Sheriff Hendrix fully in the chest. He lurched backward out of the doorway and fell to the cold ground, dead.

Almost immediately, a second shotgun blast slammed into

Wiley Mashburn. It split his face almost in two and knocked his left eye out of its socket. He staggered backward and collapsed near a small pile of wood outside the kitchen door, his unfired pistol falling beside his right hand. Virgil said later, "I could see pieces of Wiley's flesh leave his face and fly through the air." Against all odds, he did not die for several hours. Pellets from this same blast hit Frank Pike's arm.[14]

Although Pike failed to see anyone, he later testified that after the second shot someone inside the house "hollered out, 'throw down those guns—come in here or we'll shoot.'" By his account, he "went around front, hollered that they'd got both sheriffs and got behind a tree." The police officers now repeatedly fired their revolvers into the house.

Owen Brown ran out of ammunition and ducked behind a tree. Virgil Johnson later testified that after Wiley and the sheriff fell, "they [the Youngs] shot several more times. One of them got me in the ankle and I ran around to the front of the house and shot my gas gun into the place again," and again that shell hit a window frame.[15] From behind a large maple tree less than fifty feet from the house, Tony barked orders, "Hey, Charley, get away from that little tree." As he was yelling, a bullet from an upstairs window plowed through Charley's head. Sid Meadows stood behind another maple tree, just to the right of Charley, watching the back of the house. Out of ammunition, he poked his head around the tree, and a bullet drilled a hole through the center of his forehead, just as in his brother's dream.

Owen stood at the corner of the house as Ollie Crosswhite "lit a hand grenade and threw it through a front window," with no effect. Ollie, by then also out of ammunition, crawled toward the supposed safety of the storm cellar behind the house. At first, rifle shots (probably delivered by Jennings) from inside the house missed Ollie, only one making a hole through the crown of his Stetson. Finally, a shotgun blast (probably delivered by Harry) at "close range," according to the coroner, "entered the cranial cavity to destroy the brain."[16]

Tony Oliver yelled to Virgil to "go for help and ammunition." Ben Bilyeu and R. G. Wegman were already scrambling into the back seat of the police car parked at the gate. As Virgil testified, "As I got in the car I could see a man in the front room raise a rifle to his shoulder and fire at me. He shot the windshield out of the car as I was getting into it." Virgil drove off, still thinking that only Sheriff Hendrix and Deputy Mashburn had been killed.

Tony Oliver ordered Pike and Brown, out of ammunition like the rest, to the barn. Brown testified that after Hendrix and Mashburn fell, Meadows, Oliver, Houser, and Pike, as well as he, "were shooting from behind trees into the house." All this shooting had no observable effect on the besieged gunmen inside. However, shotgun pellets from the house had repeatedly knocked bark from the large soft maple where Tony was standing. Finally, pellets pierced his overcoat. Tony stepped to his right, and a rifle bullet tore through his right shoulder. As he turned toward the parked police car, firing his pistol, a second rifle bullet tore through his back. The coroner and ballistics expert, Dr. Stone, would add, "thence into the lower lobe of left lung and on through the pulmonary connections near the heart."[17]

It was Owen Brown who would later describe Tony's death. He may have been correct in the sequence of events that he related, but he was sorely inaccurate in details. For example, he stated that the chief "almost dropped his rifle," when it is a fact that the policemen carried only pistols. It was the Young brothers, unfortunately for the police, who had the rifles. (Later, in another fateful shootout, the situation would be reversed, and the police would have the rifles while the Youngs would have only pistols.) Brown said, "The men in the house were firing from the upper and lower floors and every time they'd fire you could see the lace curtains billow out through the holes in the window pane. All of a sudden the Chief sort of staggered and almost dropped his rifle. He said, 'Boys, I'm hit.' Then he got out from behind the tree and turned to our car, standing in front of the house. He staggered again, then, and I guess he must have been hit again, but he went on until he finally came to the car. Then his knees buckled, he fell over on his face beside the car. He was dead right then. He had been shot twice in the chest by rifle bullets."[18]

Now the only law enforcement officers who were still alive on the scene were Frank Pike and Owen Brown. Both of them were out of ammunition.

This is Frank Pike's description of what happened next, quoted less than four months later in *True Detective Magazine:* "We talked it over and decided we had just one chance—a dash across the open. We had been under fire three-quarters of an hour and it was getting dark."[19] Frank told the story again, twenty-three years later, in the December issue of *Men,* quoted by Duane Yarnell: "You ever watch a jackrabbit run from a hound? That's the way I ran. A couple steps ahead, then a sharp step to right or left. My break must have taken them by surprise, for I'd covered the first dozen yards before they opened up. Then it was murderous. Rifle bullets whined past my head and shotgun fire ripped away the cold ground under foot." Owen caught up with Frank in the last lap of the 250-yard run from the Young house to Haseltine Road. There they waited for reinforcements.[20]

This meant that for the next fifteen to thirty minutes there was not a single law enforcement officer on the Young farm. The place was left to the gunmen, and they took advantage of the fact to prepare for an escape.

Harry and Jennings dragged Sheriff Hendrix's body into the kitchen and took one of his guns. They, too, were running low on ammunition and needed more. They collected Ollie Crosswhite's personalized pearl-handled pistol, Wiley Mashburn's buckhorn revolver, and the guns of Tony Oliver and Sid Meadows, as well as one of Houser's guns. One pistol was recovered from Charley Houser's holster. These pistols were later to be found in a bedroom and bathroom in Houston. The rifles that the Young brothers used weren't there, having already been discovered in a deserted stolen car and returned to Springfield, where they were identified as Oscar's.

Meanwhile, Virgil Johnson, Ben Bilyeu, and B. G. Wegman had made their way back to police headquarters. There the first people they met were Sam and Otto Herrick, automobile salesmen, who were parked on Market Street. Virgil dashed inside and grabbed what arms and ammunition he could find in the police station. Police chief Ed Waddle listened with horror as he heard what had happened.

For Waddle the next hours and days blended into one long nightmare. He was almost constantly on the telephone. Reporters from the radio and the press demanded descriptions of the Young brothers and details of their flight. Rumors poured in from Oklahoma and Texas. The police chief called Governor Henry S. Caulfield and asked that the National Guard be sent in. He also requested artillery to shell the Young house and permission to bomb the Young farmhouse from the air. Governor Caulfield, noted for his prudence (having been a judge), advised Chief Waddle to exercise his best judgment, since he was on the scene and in charge. The request for National Guard troops was granted. Within two hours the artillery battery stationed in Springfield had arrived on the scene. The men directed traffic in the melee and searched fields and caves for the culprits.[21]

Virgil Johnson, with Ben Bilyeu, Sidney Kemp, detective Lee Jones (who had finished his barbering chores), and motorcycle officer Cecil McBride, sped back to the Young farm. They were the first reinforcements to arrive. Kemp took the wounded Frank Pike to a doctor. In another car were constable Scott Curtis, his son Howard, and John Hays and his son Warren (who would become chief of police in 1940).[22]

The scene was becoming crowded. Ambulances began to arrive from three different funeral homes: Fox, Starne, and Herman Lohmeyer. News of the massacre, with descriptions of Harry and Jennings Young, was being broadcast on the radio. In no time, dozens—finally hundreds—of citizens, armed with every possible weapon, began to appear at the Young farm.

Still, there was no acknowledged leader, order, or agreed-upon action. Disorganized pandemonium took over. In the January 3 *St. Louis Post-Dispatch* Frank Rhoades, Springfield's first investigative reporter, noted, "Reinforcements stopped a quarter of a mile from the farm house." There was "an hour and a half of consultation and consideration" before the disorganized posse moved into the area.[23] In the *Springfield Leader* Edward Eddy (Max Boyd) reported from the scene that finally "no man stood nearer than a hundred yards of the buildings—the house ahead of them to their left, looming dimly in the twilight, the dusk or bulk of the barn ahead to their right. There was no leader—none to shout a rallying cry for a rush into the graveyard of unburied dead."[24]

Officer Cecil McBride and Sam Herrick did at last venture up the lane to the rear of the barn. There, Sam heard a voice and a low whistle to a dog and "the weeds a-poppin'." He ran back to the crowd. McBride crouched low, "and pretty soon I seen two men comin' at me. I found my rifle wouldn't work so I got out my six-shooter. The dog with them started to growl and bark. Then I shot and one of the men said, 'Oh, my God.' He started to run and fell on his face. The other man began shooting with an automatic rifle. He threw up dirt all around me." Cecil concluded, "The man then got away when nobody would come to his aid in response to his call." Days later a morgue photograph of Harry would show a bullet hole through the palm of his right hand.[25]

Now, not knowing, of course, that the Young brothers had escaped, the leaderless mob milled around the yard of the Young farm. Everyone devised his own method of getting near the house. Frank Rhoades described the scene: "Picked men wriggled through the barbed wire fence and others dashed across open spaces and hid behind trees and bushes." The melee made for strange groupings. One band of unarmed men was made up of reporter Frank Rhoades, burly building contractor Ralph Langston, and the Youngs' neighbor, turkey farmer "Bun" Barrett.[26] Detective Lee Jones and a former newsman, Lon Scott, stood together nearby. Scott would later graphically report the advance on the dark and vacant house.

Lon Scott knew from military training that "the first thing in attacking a stronghold was a reconnoiter of the surroundings." With this in mind, he decided that he could "make a quick dash to the pole pile." He had a "high-powered rifle" and a band of ammunition over his shoulder. He crouched and ran. "Within 75 feet I stumbled by stepping on my overcoat and fell face down in a prone position." He lay still for a moment, to get his breath, and "heard some man making a sound 'uhmm.'" After ten or fifteen minutes, "with the rifle cocked and aimed at the poles," he yelled in the direction of the repeated sound, "Hey!" There was no answer; only the monotonous "uhmm, uhmm." He yelled again and Lee Jones called to him, "Is that you, Scott?" Lon shouted, "A man has me covered at the pole pile." Here, opinions differ on what happened next. According to Lee Jones's version, Lon shouted, "How much guts have you got?" Lee: "By God, as much as you have, why?" Lon's version was that it was Lee's proposal to "make a cover back to the poles." Lon said, "I'm willing to try it if you are." Lee responded, "By God, I'll go. How will we make the run?"

In any case, Grover White and officer Roscoe Gaylor joined them, and the four crawled toward the pole pile inside the barbed wire fence. "We got out of breath on our hands and knees." Again, there was the odd "uhmm" sound, repeated again and again. They crept nearer and, in front of them, they saw a man "sitting outside the kitchen door swaying forward and backward." It was Wiley Mashburn, "who kept passing his left hand to his face and saying 'uhmm.'" Lon and Lee shouted for help to come from below the hill. The only response was, "Go to hell!"

Now the lane was "afire with automobile lights." Officer Waite Phillips and reporter Frank Rhoades approached just as an ambulance arrived. Wiley was taken to Springfield Baptist Hospital, where he died.

Lon and Lee walked to the back door of the house and "stumbled onto Ollie Crosswhite." As Lon reported, "There was much pandemonium where the bodies of officers Meadows, Houser and Oliver had been found." Then "the mob was on the porch, breaking in doors." [27]

The bodies of the slain officers were loaded into the ambulance. The frustrated, milling crowd had turned into a furious mob of three to four hundred men. Finding no one to direct their fury toward, the mob vented its anger on the house. "Windows and doors were torn away and fire set to bed clothing and other furnishings."

The *Daily News* fancifully reported "a network of subterranean passages between house and barn, house and orchard, and barn and orchard made possible the escape." When Willie was questioned about the phantom caves and caverns, she was understandably astonished. [28]

Now someone in the mob yelled, "Oh, hell, let's burn the place." Edward Eddy reported, "A mattress was dragged to the porch and set afire. Brisk flames danced against the white boards. Feet stamped out the little flames." More and more people were demanding that the house be burned to the ground. Constable Scott Curtis, however, intervened. He shouted to be heard, "Don't burn the house. It's full of evidence and the killers have got away."

He ignored the fact that he was outside his jurisdiction, and yelled, "I'm deputizing everyone of you men with rifles and shotguns or any other guns. We've got to spread out through these corn fields and find the killers." Some of the growing mob obeyed him and spread out into the field, but some stayed at the house, continuing to pillage. Along with an inaccurate headline in its "extra" of January 2, "Desperadoes Slay Sheriff, Three More," the *Leader* included an obscure item tucked away on page five: "Scott Curtis Files for Sheriff's Job, First on Record." [29]

The newspaper described the scene: "The house . . . was in wild disorder. Soggy dirty feathers were on the porch and more in the small entrance way—somebody had torn open a feather mattress and the tick lay slung in a corner of what was once a living room. The upheaval was complete, not a drawer, cupboard or closet or place of any kind which had not been opened and ransacked for whatever evidence they might contain. The upright piano [from Oklahoma days] and stove in the kitchen were about the only things which stood apparently where the family had placed them."[30]

In a traveling bag and suitcase found in a bedroom was a quantity of new merchandise: "shoes, stockings, socks, shirts and a suit." These were later to be identified by Marshfield merchant S. C. Hoover as stolen from his burglarized store on October 26.[31] This was the only incriminating evidence found in the house. Contrary to popular rumor, there were no carpets piled one on top of the other on the floor. Also in the suitcase was "a Christmas gift box of handkerchiefs with a card, 'To Jennings from Nell and Vinita.'"

Among the debris in the looted house, someone found a copy of Vinita's high school yearbook, the *Resume,* for 1928 and reported that it was signed by an unusually large number of classmates. One boy wrote, "Vinita, you are a mighty fine girl and a real sport. You are one that I will never forget." Another called her "a keen looking girl and I'll bet a real sport—and everyone likes a sport."

A few days later, a local newspaper reported someone's finding, in a copy of Robert Louis Stevenson's *Travels with a Donkey,* a clipping from a newspaper with a photograph of Rudolph Valentino and his obituary. A reporter unearthed a cache of Vinita's personal letters from a number of boyfriends. From these relatively innocent artifacts, the press manufactured sensational headlines: "Vinita Young Giddy Seeker of 'High Life,'" "Love Letters of Slayers' Sister Reveal Amazing Contrasts of Character," "Fraternity Men, Traveling Salesmen and Others Figured in Romance." Needless to say, the stories did not support the lurid headlines.[32]

It was now about one o'clock in the morning, and, as someone rekindled the fire, a "partly burned purse was found in the stove in the kitchen containing two five-dollar gold pieces, a 50-cent piece and four pennies." It was assumed that the coins came from Sheriff Hendrix's clothes.

A light rain began to fall on the scene early Sunday morning. In no time, the scattered rubble lay in mud. Belatedly, Dr. Stone, in his dual capacity of coroner and temporary sheriff, ordered the farmhouse "boarded up to prevent loss of personal property and evidence from it." Willie had pleaded that the livestock be taken care of, and he ordered that this be done.[33] Nevertheless, as reported by the morning *Daily News*, "an unbroken caravan of every size and description stretched from Springfield to the Young farm." Highway patrolmen and legionnaires "fought to keep a constant stream of traffic flowing." Airplanes circled overhead.[34] Claud Pike, Frank's father, led a far-ranging squad in fruitless pursuit of clues at the homes of relatives.[35]

On January 8, 1932, a busy day for the harassed County Court, a total of eight individuals, supplementing their small depression incomes, submitted accounts for $3 a day "as guards on the Young farm," a total of $42. The "guards" included Shelby Raney and W. L. Starne, an ambulance driver. Restaurateurs Barrett and Firestone were allowed $11.95 from the Contingent Fund for providing "food for guards at Young farm."[36]

In spite of everyone's belated efforts, Harry and Jennings had escaped. To this day no one knows the precise route of their getaway. It is generally thought that they walked west across the cornfield to the west hedge fence and south past the Conn farm (home of Mrs. Oscar Young's family) to the highway. It is presumed that after Cecil McBride's shot they couldn't reach either the stolen automobile or Lorena's car, which were left in the barn. Even if they had, it would have been fruitless to try to drive down the lane, crowded as it was with members of the posse. No one knows how they got the six or more miles into Springfield. But they did.

Immediately, the radio broadcast what meager details were known. Soon the three newspapers in Springfield came out with extra editions, to the fourth and fifth extra, as new bits of information and new rumors poured in. By the morning of January 3, the massacre was front-page headline news across the nation. Unaware of Houston's impending intimate involvement with the Young affair, editors of the *Houston Chronicle* headlined, "Desperadoes Slay Six Officers in Fight," in their Sunday, January 3 edition. Inevitably, since the paper was reporting on the Ozarks, the headlines had a distinctly rural flavor: "Killers Flee to Hills During Siege of Farm House by Armed Posse." The second sentence of an Associated Press report was, "The slayers, believed to be three in number, escaped to the hills after a two-hour battle."[37] In its final Sunday edition, the *Houston Post-Dispatch* headlined, "Gunmen Flee after Slaying Six Cops." Sub-headlines were "Missouri Officers Are Mowed Down as House Stormed" and "National Guardsmen and Posses Scouring Ozarks for Fugitive Desperado and Companions After Bloody Battle at Springfield Farm."[38]

Even as the headlines were being written, the Young brothers were seeking refuge in Houston, and soon the national headlines would come from that city.

Interest shifted to Texas when a wrecked Ford coupe was found in that state. It was soon identified. Somehow the Young brothers had traveled from the Young farm to the corner of Jefferson and Commercial Streets in Springfield, where car dealer Harry Rogers had a parking lot. Rogers reported that "the car was stolen sometime between dark and 9:50 Saturday night." The official license (found in a field in Streetman, Texas) and the registered motor number absolutely identified the car used by Harry and Jennings to escape.[39]

Prosecuting attorney Dan Nee and his staff, Jim Hornbostel and Charley Chalender, felt harassed and frustrated. They were convinced that only Harry and Jennings were involved, but still the rumors would not die that there were more people inside the Young house. It seemed inconceivable that two mere small-time operators could create such havoc.[40]

Eyewitness accounts did not agree at the time and were even more unreliable years later when the survivors were interviewed. They all testified under oath at a loosely conducted coroner's inquest into the death of the six policemen. It may be that their testimony was taken by a court reporter. In any case, records of the inquest were long lost in the clutter of the basement at the Greene County courthouse and were only recently brought to light. The verdict of the coroner's jury and the coroner's official report as to the cause of death were printed in all the papers.

The most sensational testimony at the inquest came from Ben Bilyeu. He was quoted in the *Daily News:* "The man I saw in the lower building was the man they've pictured for killing Sheriff Kelly" [of West Plains]. That man was the notorious Fred Barker.[41] Frank Pike insisted to the end that he "heard the voice" of a third person—although he never saw anyone, not even the Youngs, who were there, of course. The coroner's jury of six citizens found that all six officers came to their death "at the hands of Harry Young and others unknown to this jury."[42]

The guns found in the Ford coupe in Streetman, Texas, were returned to Springfield. Oscar, in a posed photograph, held them by the barrels in each hand and identified them as his. It was established that only those two guns killed all six officers.[43]

Prosecuting attorney Dan Nee, who conducted the inquest for coroner Stone, found from all the most credible testimony that there were only two men in the house and that those two men fired all the shots. Dr. Stone, who was proud of his hobby as an amateur ballistics expert, made a "microscopic examination of marks left upon the empty shells which were picked up inside the Young farmhouse." The shells were all either 25.20 rifle cartridges or 12-gauge shotgun cartridges. Combining his amateur talent and considerable scientific knowledge, Dr. Stone reported, "Examination of the shells found in the house and the wounds which killed the six officers convinces me that only two weapons were used." His conclusion: "All indications are that only Harry and Jennings Young did the killing." Coroner Stone closed the inquest by reading into the record a description of each man's bullet wounds.[44] Testimony was reopened a few minutes later to put Lewis M. Canady on the stand. (He had driven a Herman Lohmeyer ambulance to the scene of the shooting.) Canady said that as he drove into the farm yard, the light of his ambulance rested on the barn for a moment, during which time a man ran out of the barn, vaulted a fence, and disappeared into a cornfield. Canady's glimpse of the man was too short, he said, for him to give a description.[45]

There was, the *Springfield Leader* reported, "prolonged grilling" of Lorena, Vinita, Willie, Oscar and his wife, and Lorena's hapless, good-humored husband, Albert. Albert and Willie were taken into custody as they waited for "the girls" and worried at the Smith home, not even knowing that Lorena and Vinita had been arrested. The only female in the Springfield Police Department, kind and understanding Margarite Hull, took temporary custody of Lorena's daughter, Natalie, and her dolls.[46]

A search was put out for Paul Young. He was nowhere to be found.

Vinita and Lorena were interviewed by a reporter in the dingy city jail, "fresh and alert Monday, despite their all-night interviews with cross-examiners." Lorena loved sports, she said. "I'm a good swimmer." She played the piano by ear and loved good movies. Norma Shearer and Greta Garbo were her favorites, but "I can't see what everybody's raving so about this Clark Gable for." Vinita, described as "more sprightly" than her sister this morning, "laughed about the cold potatoes brought her for breakfast." Both girls pleaded with their interviewer to "tell Mom to bear up" and to let her know that they were all right.[47]

Oscar and his wife were taken into custody on Sunday

morning at 8:30 by Sheriff Marcell Hendrix's friend and deputy Ernest Hodge. Oscar's wife, invariably referred to, even in legal documents, as "Mrs. Oscar," was bewildered and innocent of any wrongdoing. She worried about her children. She could not understand why no one would believe the simple truth. She pleaded with officers simply to check. They would find easily where both she and her husband were at the time of the shooting. Deputy Hodge declared that they were held "under the technical charge of investigation for 20 hours," and, if advisable, they would be "re-arrested and held another 20 hours."[48]

Dan Nee explained to the press that only Harry and Jennings would be charged with the murder of the six officers, "but he wanted to be prepared for any turn the case might take." Because of the guns, which were Oscar's, and because of their 2:30 visit to the farm, Oscar and his wife were to be charged as accessories before the fact (now no longer a separately described offense).

Lorena, Albert, Vinita, and Willie were to be charged with receiving stolen property, Vinita and Lorena specifically with the stolen Ford coupe that they had tried to sell to Clyde Medley. Assistant prosecuting attorney Charles L. Chalender filed an affidavit for a state warrant for Willie's arrest in the justice of the peace court of D. E. Holman. The stolen property she was charged with "receiving" was the clothing found in the suitcase and bag. The justice of the peace found "probable cause," and bond was provided for Willie by her daughters Florence and Etta Smith; on May 16, 1932, that charge was, of course, *nolle pross*ed. On January 7, Oscar and his wife were charged, in an elaborate indictment, as "accessories before the fact of murder." Mrs. Oscar was immediately released on bond. After a few days that charge was dismissed.[49]

11

WORD GOES OUT:
"FIND THE KILLERS"

In the entire sad saga of the Young family, perhaps the greatest tragedy was Willie's. Innocent, a good, religious woman, a devoted mother, a hardworking farm wife with both the skills and limitations of that role, she found herself caught up in a train of events that left her homeless and grieving. All that she had hoped and worked for was ruined; her family had become nationally infamous. She was inconsolable.

Just how and when Mom was alerted to what had gone on at her farm between the hours of three and eight o'clock on January 2, 1932, is not clear. When, to her utter astonishment, she was first taken to jail and questioned, the police were merely trying to find out which, and how many, of her sons were at the farm. At that point, they were only interested in finding and arresting automobile thieves and in breaking up what was rumored to be a nationwide conspiracy and ring of car thieves.

Knowing nothing of these matters, Willie could not comprehend why she was being held in a smelly cell of the women's section of the Greene County Jail. The police questioned her about the rumored secret caves and labyrinths leading from her house to her barn, and "the white-haired mother of the desperadoes" was said to "grow hysterical."

Assistant prosecutor Jim Hornbostel confirmed that questioning her was very difficult: "She was so wracked and exhausted from crying that she could hardly understand or answer questions." A reporter described Willie Florence Young on the morning of January 4 when jailer Wiley led her from her cell: "She wore a figured dark blue dress, and a scarf pinned around her neck as if to keep her warm. A piece of old jewelry held it together, and brown and gold beads hung around her neck. Gray hair with streaks of black was pulled back into a tight knot on her neck and very blue eyes looked at the people to whom she talked when she choked up and dropped her head."[1]

On the third day, Monday, Mom learned that her sons had killed six law enforcement officers and wounded three more in a siege at her farmhouse. Now she became truly hysterical, sobbing, unbelieving, trying to find some possible reason for the horror. "If Harry killed people like they say, he was crazy like he was ten years ago when we lived down at Ozark." When the Youngs were living in Ozark, Harry "had a crazy spell," she said. "He said all of a sudden that Clarence, my son-in-law was comin', that he knew, and when I asked him how he knew he burst out crying. He talked about how he wanted to be buried there, too, and knocked window glasses out of doors, and bent the dipper. We had to confine him six weeks."[2]

A next-door neighbor in Ozark, a teenage boy, had been an inadvertent witness to one of Harry's fits of unaccountable behavior. The boy was playing in his yard one day when he noticed Harry, barefoot, in blue overalls and blue shirt (the unofficial uniform of Ozark farm boys of the day), as he walked across his yard. Suddenly there was a piercing, shrieking yell, and Harry leaped several steps and fell on the ground on his belly, kicking and pounding the ground with his fists and bare feet.[3] Years later, a clinical psychologist, hearing these reports of Harry's "crazy spells," hazarded the opinion that he might have been a victim of psychomotor epilepsy.[4]

When these accounts were called to Vinita's attention years later, she not only expressed doubt as to the accuracy of the reports but rather firmly insisted that such episodes never occurred. This is the only known occasion on which she contradicted Mom or cast doubt on anything she said or did.

The reporter who was interviewing Willie in Springfield

did not attempt verbatim quotation after her revelation about Harry, but instead narrated the interview: "She thinks he's still a good boy at heart in spite of all the worry he's caused her. Tears welled in her eyes as she said, 'He bought me a $1 bill for a Christmas present when he came back that time.'"

Harry had gone through eighth grade at the Brick School. "He didn't want any more education," Willie said. The reporter went on to observe that the other boys too still had the love of their mother, although she was afraid that Paul and Jennings and Harry hadn't done just right "since their daddy died 10 years ago." Jennings had graduated from high school.[5] Furthermore, with obvious pride Mom reported, "Paul was the educated one. He liked to read and went three years to Phillips University." This family legend endured. However, the rather unclear records from the registrar's office at Phillips University in Enid, Oklahoma, show that James Paul Young, Presbyterian, "lived in Frederick" and "attended Phillips College Prep High School in the fall of 1916, probably for one full year."[6]

Reminded that her house had been devastated, Willie moaned, "I got no home to go to even if I get out of this awful place. They say they tore everything up. I don't know what they want to do that for." Mr. Wiley, the jailer, had told her that they had even burned the davenport that "I paid $135 for." "I don't have nothin' to live for, my home's gone, if my home's gone I don't want to be there either."

As she was led back to her cell, she appealed to the reporter: "Tell the girls I'm worried but I'll try to hold up!" She sank back on her cot. As for her daughters Lorena and Vinita, she told a reporter, "If no girls ever caused their mother more trouble than mine have, mothers would be happy."[7]

Once it was clear that Harry and Jennings had escaped, activity shifted from the farm to the police station and the office of the prosecuting attorney. From those offices came the frantic search for clues and the often fruitless attempts to find reliable information about the Young brothers' whereabouts. Law officers hoped desperately to find, quickly, the facts about exactly which desperadoes were involved and to capture them as soon as possible. The public was noisily clamoring for results.

The public, in fact, was a hindrance rather than a help in the search. On Monday morning alone, the *Daily News* reported, a "crowd of 1,000 jammed Market Street Police Station."[8] Reports of the Young brothers began to pour in from Kansas City and many other places in Missouri, from Parsons and Wichita, Kansas, as well as from Picher, Oklahoma, and other areas in that state.

The Springfield law officers were not experienced in dealing with so much "information." Chief Waddle and prosecuting attorney Nee and his staff did their best to sift through and respond to all these calls. Overwhelmed, they asked the help of law enforcement officers throughout Missouri, Kansas, and Oklahoma.

Frank Wiley, the jailer, reported the most eerie telephone call of all those received. A newspaper reported that he had "revealed today" an anonymous caller from Kansas City who asked "how many was killed in the shooting?" Wiley was absolutely certain that "the voice was much like that of Harry Young whom he had kept in jail more than once."[9]

Squads of local officers interrogated all known friends and associates of the Youngs. Farms, woods, and the caves that are common in the region were thoroughly searched. No clue turned up. The *St. Louis Post-Dispatch* reported that bloodhounds were put on the trail of the murderers at a house four or five miles from the murder scene. "They bayed lustily and started off through the woods back of the house, followed by a posse of about 40. This looked like a hot trail indeed." The hot trail ended at a farmhouse where the occupants, ten or twelve people, "had heard the hue and cry. It developed here . . . that the hounds had been following the scent of a woman who had walked through the woods a short time before. That cut down the confidence of the posse in the bloodhounds considerably."[10]

The ill-fated search was interrupted by several matters of precedence. First, it was necessary to perform the autopsies. The coroner's inquest was held at 7:30 Monday. Also, there were funerals to attend. All these events demanded attention from all officials. Upon the death of Sheriff Hendrix, Dr. Murray C. Stone, the coroner, by virtue of his office (ex officio), temporarily became the sheriff of Greene County. He was a very busy man for the next two days, filling the duties of both offices.

The Greene County Court met early Monday morning, declared the office vacant, and appointed as sheriff Maud Hendrix, the deceased sheriff's wife, until a called election could be held on January 26. At noon that day, despite the fact that her husband's funeral was scheduled to take place only the next afternoon, "the grief-stricken woman" took the oath of office and immediately reappointed the existing staff of deputies. On Thursday the Republican County Committee, under the leadership of chairman Arthur M. Curtis, nominated Mrs. Hendrix as candidate for sheriff at the special election. (Tony Oliver was to have been the Democratic party's nominee.)[11]

Law officers were having great difficulty finding "hard evidence." Furthermore, they could not yet piece together any meaningful pattern of events. The leads from far-flung places came in one at a time; the evidence accumulated only piecemeal.

One piece of evidence did turn up on Monday morning, officers revealed, in a second search of Oscar's house. Jennings had left a note on the dining room table. It read, "Give these keys to Lorena and tell her to move the cars at once."[12] At that time three automobiles rested in the barn at the Young farm—two of them stolen by Harry and Jennings in Texas. The third car in the garage was the one in which Lorena, Albert, and their daughter, Natalie, had arrived from Houston.

It was in Lorena's car that Vinita and Lorena took Mom, Natalie, and Albert into Springfield on the morning of the massacre. There they left Albert in the business district and Mom and Natalie at the Smith home, with the agreement that they were all to meet later. The two sisters then went back to the farm. They left Lorena's car there and took one of the stolen cars back into town to try to sell it, and thus the chain of events leading directly to the massacre was set in motion.

When Harry and Jennings escaped from the farmhouse after the massacre, the two cars in the garage that they were unable to get to were Lorena's and the second stolen car. The ultimate disposition of all these automobiles is unknown.

All the evidence that prosecutor Nee could find led him to conclude that Harry would be most likely to return to Houston, where he had worked while he was a fugitive for two years. Accordingly, Nee telegraphed detective lieutenant Anthony Margiotto in that city, giving the names and addresses of Harry's relatives.

One unfortunate, and innocent, person uncovered by this process was Florence, another Young sister. As reported by the *Houston Chronicle* on Monday, she was rousted out at 4 A.M. "She's a willowy girl [actually age 31] with blue eyes and light brown wavy hair. Her eyes were red from lack of sleep. Monday morning when she came to the door of the trim stucco bungalow where she lives with her husband, clad in brilliant flowered lounging pajamas she stood in the door of her home and told of her family in Missouri." She pleaded: "I sure wish there was some way my name could be kept out of the paper. You see, there's my church."

Actually, Florence could give little useful information about her brothers. She could only say, "The boys never came by to see me much. They were out here a week or two before Christmas—just for a little while." Margiotto interrupted, "And your Mother, where is she?" "Her eyes clouded, 'I don't know, now that all this has happened.'"[13]

In a few days Florence's older sisters, Gladys and Mary Ellen, would arrive in Springfield to comfort and help Mom, Lorena, and Vinita in their terrible troubles. Shortly, Florence, too, would come to Springfield to take care of necessary business matters. It was she who would sign the required bonds and see that the farm was disposed of.

Houston police officers, said to be "taking their cue from the French maxim 'Cherchez la Femme' (search for the woman)," combed the city Sunday night for the saleswoman whom they believed to be the recently married Mrs. Harry Young.[14] Under a front-page headline, the *Houston Chronicle* described this episode: "The officers laid siege Monday morning to a cottage at 1003 Terminal Street but when they entered the place they did not find the Youngs." The house was believed to be where Harry and his new bride resided. "The girl, Florence Calvert, was reported to have married the killer three weeks ago.

"Officers surrounded the house early Monday morning. For several minutes they circled the building, knocking on the doors and calling for the people inside to come out. Shortly after 9 A.M. detectives entered the house and found the remains of a breakfast that appeared to have been made for two. They took into custody a sister of Young's bride. She was taken to the police station for questioning. The sister said that Florence had gone to the Medical Arts Building to see her doctor following a minor mouth operation. Detective C. V. (Buster) Kern hastened to the surgeon's office. The girl had not appeared at noon Monday."[15]

After this unfruitful foray, detective lieutenant Beverly led a squad to a house on Avenue I in another search for the new bride. Tear gas was fired into the attic. The *Houston Post-Dispatch* reported: "Detective C. V. Kern mounted a fragile ladder and climbed into the upper story with drawn pistol as he prepared to meet the desperate Missourians. The attic was empty."

Moving in closer, perhaps even on the heels of Harry, at least, at noon on Monday, "a milk wagon driver with whom Harry had worked notified officers that he had seen Harry in the 6500 block of Avenue I as he called at the home of his wife. A neighbor, recognizing Harry, followed him to the Harrisburg bus line two blocks away." The bus driver could not tell officers where he got off the bus, but he did say that a man fitting Harry's description had boarded the bus at the corner that the neighbor described. The *Houston Post-Dispatch* concluded: "Like a phantom, the elusive killer of the Ozark hills appeared in another section of Magnolia Park, residents told officers, but the rough search of the vicinity failed to reveal any trace of the ex-convict."[16]

A broader search began. "Detectives were detailed to guard every railway and bus station, every airport, highway and wharf. Guards were posted along the Rio Grande; Adjutant-General Sterling ordered Texas rangers to be on the lookout." There were proposals to search ships. (As the *Springfield News* reported, "It was feared he might have stowed away on an outgoing vessel.") The Houston paper said, "The waterfront, long considered a stronghold of 'wanted men' had been raked with a fine-tooth comb by 2 A.M. Tuesday without a trace of the desperadoes." One commentator noted, "What is perhaps the greatest man hunt of Houston's history got under way at dawn Monday."[17]

While the frantic pursuit of Harry and Jennings was in progress in Houston, members of the local Missouri press continued to confront Vinita and Lorena in the dingy Springfield jail and the distraught Willie in a county jail cell. The beleaguered women had certainly not sought this publicity. On the contrary, they were dismayed. Sadly, they seemed to be under the embarrassing impression that they were obliged by some public duty to respond. Neither they nor their tormentors had ever heard of anything so elementary as the rights to silence and counsel.

When they were arrested on Saturday, Lorena and Vinita "denied knowledge that the boys were near and said no one was at home when they left with their mother." As they were photographed in the city jail, well-dressed in attractive poses with wry smiles, it was reported that "they have been severely grilled in an effort to obtain information of their brothers."

On Sunday night they were put in separate cells. Steadfastly, Vinita stood by her story and refused to implicate her brothers. Finally, questioners confronted her with information from her sister and mother that conflicted with her statements. "She finally 'kicked in' and made what she said was 'a clean breast of it all.'"

In a joint interview, declaring that they wanted to tell the truth, the sisters "apologized for telling the news reporter who obtained the first interview Saturday night that they had not seen Harry or Jennings. Vinita explained, 'You wouldn't want to get your own brothers in trouble would you? No matter what they had done?'"[18]

The fact that six law enforcement officers had been slain and three wounded at the Young farm was now national news. Reporters were greedy for details to flesh out their sidebars. Willie was taken out of her jail cell time after time to be photographed and interviewed.

On Tuesday morning the *Springfield Daily News* ran a grim photograph of the distraught woman on the front page. The accompanying article read: " 'I don't want to see my boys hang like they say will happen, and I want to be gone. I don't have nothin' to live for,' sobbed the gray-haired woman." The confused, grieving mother said, "I've tried to get the boys to go right. But now if they did this they deserve punishment." Finally, she repeated, "I can't bear to think of them hangin'. I hope they shoot themselves."[19]

Hard evidence came in bit by bit. It was never assembled or recorded in an orderly manner. To this day it cannot be accurately reproduced. Only part of the story is known.

In 1932 highways were, at best, primitive by today's standards. Allowing only for two-lane traffic, they were mostly concrete, some macadam. They meandered through every town and village from Springfield, Missouri, the 680 miles to Houston, Texas. Those highways, described as "terrible" by a Missouri highway engineer, have now been all but obliterated by intricate interstate systems.[20]

Streetman, Texas, a village of less than four hundred

inhabitants, is 511 miles from Springfield and 169 miles from Houston. It was on the outskirts of Streetman, between twelve and one o'clock Sunday, January 3, 1932, less than eighteen hours after the massacre, that a speeding Ford coupe skidded off the highway and crashed into a ditch.

The passengers, two men, one injured and bleeding, scrambled from the wreckage. They waved traffic on until a Mr. Carroll, a farmer, rode up on a horse. The two men were Harry and Jennings Young. The Ford coupe had been stolen from Harry Rogers's lot in Springfield.

One of the men asked Carroll where there was a phone and if a wrecker could be called. Carroll himself had a telephone; but, he said, there was "no nearby wrecker service." He offered to hitch up his team and pull the coupe from the ditch to a shed on his nearby farm.

By the time Carroll returned with the mules to pull the car, the men were gone. Even so, he dragged the coupe from the ditch to his farmyard, expecting the stranded motorists to return at any moment. Carroll saw a rifle and a shotgun in the coupe but supposed that the men had been hunting. Later, a celebrity for the moment, Carroll would pose in creased hat, sweater, and light-colored trousers beside the battered coupe, the rifle over his left arm, the shotgun standing on its stock.

After inspecting the guns, he noticed that the license plates were missing from the car. His daughter told him that she "had seen one of the men tear something off the auto that was hurled into the nearby field." Carroll returned to the ditch and, from the adjoining field, retrieved the Missouri license plates.

When by late afternoon the motorists had not returned and Carroll mulled over the strange events, he became suspicious and decided to "put in a call through the Streetman Exchange" for Sheriff Jim Sessions in Corsicana. Mrs. A. E. Gaddy operated the Streetman telephone exchange and, fortuitously, "overheard" the conversation between Carroll and the sheriff's office. However, she did not mention the fact of the eavesdropped conversation to her family.

The sheriff of Navarro County, in turn, called prosecutor Nee and relayed Carroll's information. This telephoned description of the guns, the license plates, and the wrecked automobile was the first hard evidence to come in.[21]

The telegram from Corsicana read: "Two men fitting description of Harry and Jennings Young wrecked Ford car Streetman, Texas, today. Disappeared immediately going toward Houston. Missouri license 363–663."

Later that afternoon A. E. Gaddy, Jr., was listening to news over radio station KMOX, St. Louis, and heard a vivid account of the massacre with detailed descriptions of Jennings and Harry Young and their brother Paul. A. E. told his mother about the broadcast, and for the first time she mentioned "overhearing" Carroll's call to Sheriff Sessions. Gaddy excitedly telegraphed the information to prosecutor Nee in Springfield. Nee immediately responded with a return telephone call. The two telegrams and telephone conversation persuaded Nee that it was, indeed, Harry and Jennings who had wrecked the coupe, and that their destination was Houston and Harry's old haunts.

A full account of the fugitives' flight was pieced together slowly, in tantalizing bits. On Monday morning E. C. Hogan, a Houston drug salesman, was in Fairfield, fifteen miles south of Streetman, having a burned-out bearing repaired on his automobile. He had heard of the massacre and learned that Texas law enforcement officers were engaged in a frantic search. He revealed that he was the man who had "picked up the injured men beside their wrecked auto at Streetman" while Mr. Carroll had gone for his mules. Hogan reported that one of the men had "seemed badly injured about the body, shoulder and hip. They talked but little; one gave the name of Chester Phillips and said he lived in Houston," and, the drug salesman said, he had "damaged his car in attempting to get the two men medical attention."

When the Hogan automobile stalled on the Caney Creek bridge, it forced Isaac Levy, described in Streetman as an "aged man" of Corsicana, to stop. Hogan stayed with his car at the time, and Levy, in turn, picked up the stranded passengers. He said that one of the men "was wearing a grey overcoat and seemed to have a neck injury. The man complained that his spine had been injured." As they proceeded down the highway, Levy said, "They offered to pay me well if I'd take them to Houston. But I was suspicious of them when the one who was injured did not want to stop at Fairfield to have his wounds dressed. I figured they had been into something and started to turn them over to Fairfield officers but decided I might be wrong and didn't do anything. I thought maybe they were going to make me drive to Houston but they didn't. I drove into a filling station at Fairfield and let them out. They thanked me for the lift."[22]

Here evidence becomes murky. One unidentified account said that they were picked up by a "cotton truck." A bystander in Fairfield said it was "by another motorist who has not been identified." To this day we do not know how Harry and Jennings got the remaining 136 miles to Houston. By one account, Harry was searching for his wife in Houston as early as three o'clock. We do know that by six o'clock Harry and Jennings had found a place to stay in Houston.

Exhausted from loss of sleep and long hours pursuing clues, prosecutor Nee and his assistant Jim Hornbostel had been persuaded by talking to Hogan and Levy that Harry and Jennings had eluded all pursuers and were in Houston. Although, in fact, the gunmen were armed with five of their victims' pistols, both Hogan and Levy assured Nee, "Neither of the killers had a single revolver or pistol upon their person and were not in possession of any traveling bags."[23]

A proofreader for the *Houston Post-Dispatch*, returning from his lunch break, was approached by a "well-dressed" man: "Say, I'm awfully anxious to read about these Missouri killers. Where can I get a midnight edition?" Jim Hatfield, age fifty-four, the accommodating proofreader, went inside and got a copy of the paper. Then he went back to prepare copy for the next edition. "Can you imagine my surprise Tuesday morning when I recognized a photograph on page one of the final edition as that of Harry Young?"[24] The *Houston Chronicle* headlined across the front page of its home edition of Monday: "Police comb Houston for 'Mass Slayers.'"[25]

A typical small business occupation of the Great Depression was to bring the massacre and the ensuing manhunt to an explosive conclusion. J. F. Tomlinson, age fifty, a carpenter, lived at 4610 Walker Street in the Eastwood section of Houston with his wife and teenage daughter, Mary Elise. Their home was a neat five-room green bungalow surrounded by evergreen trees and rose bushes. Five steps led up to the railed front porch, which had a rose trellis at the east end. A hall extended through the house from front to rear, on the left a front bedroom and a rear bedroom, a connecting bathroom between. On the right side of the hall were a living room, dining room, and a kitchen. To supplement their depression income, the Tomlinsons sometimes rented the front bedroom.

About ten o'clock Monday morning Mr. Tomlinson rented the front bedroom to two men. He knew "the little one" as Claude Walker, who once lived down the street and worked for a dairy. "The room had been vacant for weeks and he was glad to rent it." By six o'clock the two men, with one suitcase, were ensconced in the front bedroom with a dozen oranges and apples and a frosted coconut cake. That evening the Tomlinsons went to the home of a neighbor and played Forty-Two until about ten o'clock.

After they returned, "I had to look at the *Chronicle* before I went to bed." There, on the front page, under the banner headline, "Police Comb Houston for 'Mass Slayers,'" was an excellent photograph of Harry Young, "the little one," "hatless." Tomlinson realized, "It looked like the man who had rented my room. Then I got to thinking. This man I thought was Claude Walker had kept his hat on all the time—even while he was in the house. My wife and I read every word in the paper about the Young boys and what happened in Missouri. I guess we didn't sleep much that night."

Tomlinson reported, "I started to go get the officers but then I thought maybe there'd be a lot of people killed right there in my home." The Tomlinsons did not know when their roomers retired, but at 10:30 the men were quiet. The family waited to do anything until morning, when Mr. Tomlinson took Mary Elise to junior high school as usual. As he was going into the hall, "the little fellow was going out the front door," and Tomlinson became disturbed. "What if he's gone for good?" But he left Mary Elise at school and went directly to the home of chief of police Percy F. Heard. Chief Heard, "wearied by days and nights of chasing down unfounded clues," was skeptical at first; "but when the carpenter told him that his roomer's name was Walker," he immediately went into action. Rather than take the risk of alerting the news media and the curious by going to headquarters, Chief Heard summoned to his home chief of detectives Kirk Irwin and nine select officers—detective lieutenants B. W. Payne (homicide squad leader), George Peyton, and Claude Beverly; and detectives W. M. Barrett, Ira Williams, Henry Bradshaw, Bob Martin, George Lathrop, and Dave Turner. Lieutenant Anthony Margiotta and Captain Roy Young arrived just as the policemen surrounded the cottage.[26]

Because Tomlinson had been alerted to the presence of the desperate gunmen by the newspaper account of the massacre and manhunt, the editor of the *Houston Chronicle* could not resist headlining later, "Boy delivering Chronicle Began Moves that Ended in Deaths of Slayers."[27] The *Chronicle* was to describe what ensued as a "gun battle." Later there were photographs of this victorious elite, not one injured. They were photographed singly, in pairs, and in groups, some exhibiting the five pistols recovered from the bedroom and bathroom. Chief Heard was a ruggedly handsome, smiling man, of courageous leadership. The men, in their vested suits, white shirts, and ties and, always, the light-colored Stetsons tilted at becoming angles, were clearly Houston's finest.[28]

The well-armed squad assembled quickly with a sub-

machine gun and tear gas bombs, unlike the hapless Springfield law officers. These men were also well equipped with
rifles and shotguns. This time the Young brothers were
armed only with the pistols of their victims. This time they
were not in an impregnable fortress. This time they were
taken by surprise.

With the anxious carpenter, the formidable posse drove
within a block of the green cottage on Walker Avenue and
waited. Harry had returned with groceries and "crawled
back into bed with his brother." An alarmed Mrs. Tomlinson
telephoned their card-playing neighbor, E. A. Rich. "She
spoke real low with her mouth to the phone," pleading,
"come over and get me quick." Rich hurried up the street
and drove away with Mrs. Tomlinson.

Chief Heard directed the nervous carpenter to walk down
the block to reconnoiter the bungalow and make certain that
his wife was safe. He checked and reported that his wife was
gone and "the two men were asleep in the front room."
Chief Heard and his picked squad advanced and surrounded
the bungalow. Tomlinson waited in the yard, even "during
the firing."[29]

12

THE SECOND
SHOOTOUT

The Young family drama sped to its tragic climax with the relentlessness of a Greek drama. Only days after the bloody shootout with law officers at the Young farm, Harry and Jennings found themselves in another fatal confrontation.

The facts of this event are not to be found in any official records or original sources. They do not exist. It is inconceivable that the Houston Police Department in 1932 did not compile an official record of what was publicized as "the greatest man hunt in the history of Texas." Yet, inexplicably, those records, like the ones in the Springfield Police Department, have disappeared. Records of both shootouts have completely vanished, without a trace.

In 1972 an effort was made to track down the Houston records. Carol S. Vance, then district attorney of Harris County, and Bob Burdette, his executive assistant, undertook the task of trying to unearth original official files or records of the Houston police department.

On February 4, 1972, this was the terse report: "I have contacted the Houston Police Department and they advise they have no records regarding this particular case." Again, on February 23, "After diligent search, apparently the only record that exists of the Young brothers killing is a copy of the fingerprint card of Jennings Young which I enclose." That tiny artifact was a certified copy of the entry record of "Major Jennings Young—Ben G. Bowers" (an alias) from the Leavenworth Penitentiary, dated 1930. Mr. Vance also had contacted the Harris County Medical Examiner's Office as a possible source of original documentation and information.[1] Dr.

97

Joseph A. Jachimczyk, M.D., L.L.D., a forensic pathologist and lawyer reporting as medical examiner, gave this report in 1972: "The sole information which I was able to obtain comes from the Bureau of Vital Statistics of the City of Houston."[2] That sparse information was a copy of the death certificates of Harry and Jennings Young signed by justice of the peace Campbell R. Overstreet.

The only way to reconstruct the final confrontation between the Young brothers and the law on Walker Avenue on Tuesday, January 5, 1932, is through secondary sources. Those sometimes contradictory accounts abound. There are as many tales of the end of the Young brothers' lives as there were reporters and participants. A few solid facts, however, are firm. All agree, it was over in a very few minutes.

Lacking official files, the most reliable sources for an account of the last minutes in the lives of Harry and Jennings Young are the interviews that the law enforcement officers gave to news reporters.

Of those officers, detective lieutenant Claude Beverly appears to have been the most articulate. He described how the posse surrounded the bungalow: detectives Stinson and Barrett went to the rear door; Chief Heard, Peyton, and Beverly went to the front door. As this trio went up the front steps, they were startled to find a man at the front door. He was a neighbor, a painter looking for work. According to Beverly's report, they handcuffed this man, A. P. Singleton, to a tree in the front yard and "walked into the hall together." They heard no one. "Chief Heard stayed at the front door and Peyton and I went to the rear bedroom door. We opened it and tiptoed in. We went to the door which connected the bedroom with the bath. We unlatched the bathroom door.

"The door opened a little way and we jumped back into the hall. Three shots were fired, one coming into the hallway.

"Then we went to the kitchen door, across the hall, from which we had a view of the rear bedroom and the bathroom door.

"Everything was quiet for a few minutes.

"Then the bathroom door opened a few inches and one of the Young brothers peeped out.

"I fired one time with a sawed-off shotgun.

"There were four more shots in the bathroom.

"A voice called, 'We're dead—come on in.'

"I called to Stinson and told him to start firing with the tear gas. Barrett went to the bathroom window and started pouring gas into the bathroom. Stinson went to the front bedroom door and started shooting gas in there.

"We waited for the gas to clear up and then went into the bathroom and found two men—one dead and the other dying."[3]

The substance of this report was immediately printed in newspapers across the country. The *Springfield Leader* headlined: "Harry, Jennings Perish in Texas After Gun Fight."[4]

A different story, on the front page of the *Houston Chronicle*, opposite Lieutenant Beverly's interview, was given by the painter, A. P. Singleton, who, according to Beverly, had been handcuffed to a tree. The headline on this story was "Painter, Who Was Knocking on Door of Hideout, Says Cops Used Him as a Shield." Singleton said that he had rung the doorbell three times. When no one answered, he "was fixing to leave when about 10 policemen on foot, carrying shotguns, rifles and gas guns, commanded, 'who are you? Stick up your hands.'" He was surprised, and put his hands up, "but the officers were closing in on me." Always referring to the officers as "cops," he reported: "One cop pushed me in the front door and he with another man who they kept calling 'Chief' stuck a shotgun and pistol in my back. They walked me into the house and one of them said, 'Kick that door open.' I kicked but the door was locked."

Singleton tried to explain to the officers why he was at the house and pleaded, "I'm an innocent guy in here and you'd better let me go before I get shot." The response, according to Singleton: " Keep still and you won't get shot,' they said and kept nudging me with the barrels of the guns. 'Let them hands down and I'll fix you,' the fellow with the pistol said. I was in a tight spot and knew it so I reached higher."

Singleton went on, "The cop with the shotgun walked to the end of the hall where a door was open and just as he entered the room two shots were fired and then a voice said, 'Come on in, we've killed ourselves.' The fellow with the shotgun ran out of the room like a shot and just into another room across the hall. The fellow with the pistol that they called Chief nudged me with the barrel of that gun again. Finally, he went out. I followed him. There wasn't anything else to do. When I got outside I ran into a cop with a machine gun. Another one ran up and put handcuffs on my wrists and chained me to a tree. I never have been in such a predicament."[5]

Exactly what evidence, if any, justice of the peace Overstreet heard cannot be known. The only surviving scrap of official record is the laconic death certificate signed by him in his capacity to conduct an inquest. The press simply stated that he was "called to hold an inquest over the bodies," and Judge Overstreet "stated [in advance of the hearing] he would return a verdict of murder in each case." He "expressed the opinion that the brothers had entered into a suicide pact." He was quoted, "They stood face to face and shot each other. Jennings was shot seven times with Harry's gun, a 30 caliber pistol."[6]

The *Houston Post-Dispatch* reported that in addition to the four wounds that Jennings "suffered at the hands of his brother, he was wounded by three pellets from a shotgun blast. The buckshot wounds were found on the hand, head and jaw." The gun was found under Harry. Harry "was shot twice with a 44 caliber pistol which was fired by Jennings."

The certificate reads:

"Jennings Young, Age 35, Date of Death—January 5, 1932, Place of Death—4710 Walker Street, Houston, Texas, and Cause of Death—Pistol shot wounds inflicted by Harry Young—Murder.

"Harry Lyman Young, Age 27, Date of Death—January 5,

1932, Place of Death—4710 Walker Street, Houston, Texas, and Cause of Death—Pistol shot wounds inflicted by Jennings Young—Murder."[7]

Even as the inquest was reported, the first doubts about the accuracy of the verdict were being heard. After quoting Judge Overstreet and his extrajudicial opinion, the *Houston Chronicle* commented: "Whether or not their deaths were due entirely to their own weapons or partially to bullets from officers' guns was debatable. Each man was shot several times, some of the wounds, physicians said undoubtedly [were] self-inflicted. Other wounds are believed to have been from officers' bullets."

There were photographs of patrolman H. E. Goodsen, pointing to the "twelve bullet holes in the bedroom door." The report accompanying these pictures said, "Police fired a blast of lead through this door into the room where Harry and Jennings Young were cornered." The bathroom door was riddled with pellets.[8]

The *Springfield Press* printed the bylined report of Harry McCormick, headlined, "Reporter Risks Life to Get Eye-Witness Story of Climax in Youngs' Crime Career." McCormick said that Heard opened the front door "and Beverly slipped in behind it." McCormick "peered around the corner, pushed a porch chair against the screen to hold it back." And then, he reports, "there was a roar of pistol fire and I saw Beverly's gun spit fire. I saw the officers retreating. From inside the house the roar of guns came again. Then a muffled voice reached our ears, 'Come and get us, we're dead.'"[9]

The brothers were in bed as the posse surrounded the bungalow, Harry "clad only in his underwear and pants" and Jennings dressed only in his "blue silk underwear." Chief Heard was quoted as saying, "In all, the Young brothers fired about ten shots, four at officers and six at themselves." The undertaker described Harry's wounds as "a bullet hole through the palm of his left hand" and "other wounds in the heart and head were made with a .38 caliber revolver." In Harry's pants pockets were "$201.03, a pearl-handled knife and five .44 caliber Smith and Wesson pistol cartridges." The total cash found on both brothers was $269.72.[10]

The *Springfield Leader* ran a serene photograph of the entire family, a separate portrait of Willie, and an explicitly gruesome photograph of Jennings's bullet-ridden torso. The editor explained apologetically, "The Leader departs from precedent in printing this photograph. But it illustrates so vividly—a thousand times more vividly than words could illustrate—the horror and folly of crime that the Leader feels justified in its publication." Whether or not the photograph deterred anyone from the "folly of crime," it doubtless helped newspaper sales.[11]

It was in the dingy Springfield jail that Mom learned her sons were dead. She immediately plunged into despair. One newspaper headline noted, "Mother's Sobs Only Requiem for Two Men." (One is reminded of a letter of Robert Frost: "A mother can follow an erring son even to the gallows and beyond in tears to his grave in quick-time without in any way sharing in his guilt.")[12]

It was on Tuesday afternoon that Vinita and Lorena learned, secondhand, of the tragedy. They heard newsboys outside the city jail shouting "Extra" and a quarrel between a reporter seeking an interview and a guard. Thus the sisters were "informed that their brothers had been captured, dead and dying." County jailer Frank Wiley "brought Mrs. Young from the women's quarters into the small bare room adjoining when reporters arrived to break the news to her."

Beth Campbell, the newspaper's "sob sister," in the language of the day, described the scene: "The mother of the killers stood in the center of the ugly high-ceilinged room with its mustard-yellow walls. She stood quiet, apprehensive. Her white silk scarf was pulled tighter about her neck than yesterday. Her figured blue crepe dress was wrinkled from sleeping huddled on a cot chained to the wall. One hand clasped her gold and cornelian beads nervously. She looked questioningly at her visitors."

Beth Campbell said to her quietly, "Jennings and Harry

shot themselves this morning." Beth reported, "A support-ing arm felt the tremor which went through her body. She looked up wildly. 'Are?' she began. Her eyes completed the query." Beth Campbell answered the unspoken question, "Jennings is dead, Harry dying."

"Oh, my God! Oh, my God! Why did they do it? My own flesh and blood. My own flesh and blood. Lord have mercy on me. What am I to do now? I can't take my own life. I'd go down to eternal torture. Daddy's in heaven. I'm glad Daddy didn't even know about this."

Beth reported, "She would have fallen several times had it not been for persons supporting her on both sides. Her voice trailed off into hysterical nothings. She twisted a much-fin-gered handkerchief, white with a blue plaid border between her freckled, wrinkled hands, upon which she wore only one ring—a white-gold wedding band."

At last, Wiley brought a chair, and "she sank down into its hardness still clutching the arms of reporters. Her moans grew weaker, then swelled to screams in a regular tempo echoing through the rickety bare jail with a ghastly effect."[13]

In deepest grief, overwhelmed by the awful events that had ripped her life apart and shattered her dignity, she tried to find a way to describe her despair. She groped for some concrete image that would let the world know the terrible suffering and humiliation she had endured. She sobbed, the quintessential grandmother, "The worst things happened, you see, last night I took out my lower teeth and I rolled 'em up in my coat under my head, thinkin' they'd be safe. Well, this morning, I woke up and threw my coat over the door and the teeth fell out and broke. And that ain't all. Last night they put a drunk girl in there, right in the same room with us, and the liquor smelled awful and I didn't like it a bit. But my teeth's the worst. If you see my girl, Vinita, down at the city jail tell her I broke my teeth and I'd like to get 'em downtown and get 'em fixed."[14]

13

THE SURVIVORS' TALES

Reliable, comprehensive records of the Young brothers massacre do not exist. For details, the historian of this event must rely in large part on reports from survivors.

The Springfield Police Department once assembled a file concerning the massacre. It was stored in the "library" (the evidence-preservation room) of the new police headquarters. In May 1972, chief of police Sam Robards proposed a perusal of the record to an inquisitive visitor. As he carefully thumbed through the filing cabinet, he suddenly became excited and then frantic as he again fruitlessly searched the filing cabinet. Finally he exclaimed, "Well, I'll be damned, it's gone." Then he mused, "The last time I saw that file a former chief of police was sitting right here at this table going through that file and now it is not here." Thus, another baffling and curious mystery has been added to the event: the complete disappearance of an official report. We must rely on other contemporary sources to establish the facts.[1]

Memories are fragile, dimmed by time and colored by the understandable temptation to place one's self in a favorable, even a heroic, light. Also, survivors differ widely in their willingness to talk of the event. Some are modest and reticent; others are prone to exaggerate the roles they played. Simply surviving the martyrdom may have been an embarrassing burden.

Some of the survivors, especially descendants and members of the Young family who took part in the events or were closely involved with them, are honorable, innocent, and embarrassed men and women who totally disapproved of the three Young brothers and their lives of crime. The sole desire of these people has been to disassociate themselves from the event. Some, such as Harry's Texas wife of only a short time, disappeared immediately after the events and were not heard of again. Others, such as Jennings's wife, sought and achieved anonymity. She resumed her maiden name, Bessie Smith, and was for many years a popular waitress at leading hotels and restaurants in Springfield. Vinita, when asked for details of her brothers' crimes, repeatedly says, "That is something to forget."[2]

Years afterward, Frank Pike complained, "They do not seem to want a true story." Pike discounted the account given by John R. Woodside in his brochure and presented his own version in the detective story magazines of the 1930s.[3]

To this day, people are eager to assess guilt, claim bravery or courage for themselves, and point the finger of timidity at others. Still, it is this testimony on which one must rely. One man completely forgotten in the bizarre episode is R. G. Wegman, whom Woodside designated "a civilian" in his brochure. Wegman was friendly with Springfield policemen and occasionally visited the police station, chatting with the desk sergeants. Woodside says, "He climbed in to make a total of 11 men involved in what was soon known as America's worst peace officer massacre."

It is certain that Wegman was at the police station on that January afternoon and that he "climbed in" one of the police sedans. Where he was during the massacre, however, is not entirely clear. Woodside reports that Pike and "civilian" R. G. Wegman were ordered to "the rear of the officers' cars to keep careful watch of the barn and shed." Wegman rode back to the city with Ben Bilyeu in the police car driven by Virgil Johnson. That is all we know. No newspaper interviews of him exist. He has vanished completely, his role in the historic event obliterated.[4]

Four survivors who were at the scene of the massacre were Frank Pike, Owen Brown, Ben Bilyeu, and Virgil Johnson. The four policemen were grateful to have jobs in the depression years of 1931/32. They were also dedicated law officers, and each of them enjoyed a good reputation in his profession. Various sources have reported that the original posse leaving the Market Street station comprised ten law enforcement officers, of whom six were killed and four wounded. In fact, eleven people left the police station in three automobiles. Sheriff Hendrix, his deputy Wiley Mashburn, and special agent Ollie Crosswhite rode in one vehicle. Following in a police car driven by Charley Houser were Oliver, Meadows, Bilyeu, and Johnson, followed in turn by a third car carrying Pike, Brown, and Wegman.

Frank Pike was one of the more colorful survivors. Outliving all other participants, he became the best-known public figure involved in the massacre. He was very handsome, always dapper in both uniform and civilian dress, his hat brim snapped at a jaunty angle.

A newspaper photograph taken in 1943 shows him in uniform, with three guitars that he made as a hobby. When he was young, he could play any stringed instrument, and he traveled with a magician and performing troupe. Pike's father was a professional law enforcement officer, once police chief of Eureka Springs, Arkansas, and, for a time, chief of police of Springfield. In the course of his long career, Frank served as a motorcycle patrolman, a detective, and as a security officer at the United States Medical Center in Springfield, where one of his coworkers was Oscar Young. For years Pike was in charge of the city's parking meter operations.[5]

In later years his activities were curtailed by blindness. He kept alive the saga of the Young brothers massacre, especially on anniversaries of the event, which were marked in local newspapers. He had hoped to have the story made into a movie or television series; unfortunately, his dream was not fulfilled within his lifetime.

Owen R. Brown was a tall man, a career policeman—first a uniformed patrolman, and then a detective. He was a patrolmate of Lloyd "Boots" Miller, whose father was a deputy

United States marshal in 1932. When "Boots" Miller became director of penal institutions in Missouri, he brought Owen to Jefferson City. The Official State Manual for 1943/44 lists his prior employment as "Police Lieutenant" and his occupation as in the "Industrial Department" at $1,800 a year.[6]

In gathering material for his brochure, prepared a few days after the massacre, John R. Woodside relied on the accounts he gleaned from Owen Brown, Frank Pike, and Virgil Johnson. Forty years later, Pike belittled the performance of Brown, Bilyeu, and Johnson; the descendants of the slain officers, in turn, disparaged Pike's role.[7]

Pike's scornful attitude toward Woodside's brochure was still recalled in 1984. When his loyal and devoted wife Eva was offered a copy, she disdainfully answered, "Frank never liked that book; it was not that way, and he was there."[8]

Virgil Johnson was another career officer. He was always neat in appearance, correct in his behavior, and as serious as he looked. Johnson was known for his fundamentalist religious fervor. In later years he maintained a low profile. He was seldom quoted directly about the events of January 2, 1932, either involving his own part or his companions'.

One of the more interesting characters and survivors of the massacre was Ben Bilyeu. The numerous Bilyeus constituted a Christian County clan. Their ancestors were homesteaders, solid reliable farm families, and the family remains an important part of the community. Members of the Bilyeu family were always active in Christian County politics. All candidates vied for their collective support, and one officeseeker, Fred W. Barrett, said, before women could vote, that there were forty-eight Bilyeu voters and they were always against him.

Ben was thought by some to be the black sheep of the family. In February 1908, Fred W. Barrett, prosecuting attorney of Christian County, filed a complaint charging Ben and Newt Bilyeu, then mere boys, with "disturbing the peace of one C. H. Clevenger by then and there cursing and swear-

ing and by loud and unusual noises, and by offensive and
indecent conversation and by threatening, quarreling, challenging and fighting." This carefully drafted legalism is an
elaborate euphemism for disturbing a "brush-arbor"
religious meeting. Ben's bond of $100 was signed by many
friends and relatives, and upon a plea of guilty, Ben and
Newt were fined "one dollar and costs of $26.13." Possessing
no property, they petitioned for "discharge," having,
according to the law of that day, "actually served one day's
imprisonment for every two dollars of said fine and costs."[9]

More seriously, on August 21, 1917, William L. Vandeventer, the prosecuting attorney, charged Ben, Frank,
Harlan, and Lenzi Bilyeu with the murder of Frank Tabor
and in a second affidavit with "felonious assault" upon Win-
nie Hensley. The Bilyeus were defended by G. Purd Hayes,
who enjoyed the longest law career in Christian County, and
by a rising lawyer in Springfield, Roscoe C. Patterson. John J.
Moore, Fred W. Barrett, and Tom R. Moore (a former circuit
judge, later to be succeeded by his son) were special pros-
ecutors. The charges came to an inconclusive end and the
records are now incomplete. We do know that in long, bit-
terly contested criminal proceedings and after a severance of
parties, a jury found Linzi Bilyeu not guilty of murder. Ben
was never tried.[10]

Then, in July 1918, prosecuting attorney John T. Hays
(brother of G. Purd Hays) charged that Ben Bilyeu "wilfully
[sic] and maliciously [did] throw down and open a certain
fence," the property of J. J. Ingenthron. Again, Ben pleaded
guilty and was fined "one dollar and costs of suit."[11]

In Steve McLaughlin's monographs Ben is not listed as a
member of the police department. However, he had been
very active on behalf of Mayor Gideon in his campaign and
was rewarded by a place on the force.

Bilyeu was the only survivor of the massacre to say that he
recognized anyone in the Young farmhouse. He testified at
the inquest that he saw Harry fire a rifle from an upstairs
window. He also identified a photograph of the notorious

outlaw Fred Barker as the man who appeared at a downstairs window at the same moment.

Ben remained a dutiful and loyal law enforcement officer to the end of Mayor Gideon's term and was always a ward worker and force in local Republican campaigns.

14

AFTERMATH OF
DISASTER

MEMORIALS, FUNERALS

Many lives were profoundly changed by the massacre and the events that followed. Even people whose destinies were not directly involved found themselves swept along in the rapid stream of events.

On January 2, immediately after the massacre, news of the disaster spread through Springfield like a brush fire in a high wind. People gathered at the police station, waiting for every scrap of news, even before the ambulances bringing wounded and dead policemen from the Young farm had had time to return.

A siren whined in the distance, and "dozens of men and women ran to see which way it was going," to quote one of the local newspapers. This ambulance, from Herman Lohmeyer, was the first to pass the station. It was taking deputy sheriff Wiley Mashburn to a nearby hospital. There, in only a few minutes, he died.

Another ambulance, from W. L. Starne, carried the body of detective Ollie Crosswhite. Soon, a third ambulance pulled into the Fox Funeral Home. In it were the bodies of Sheriff Hendrix, detectives Tony Oliver and Sid Meadows, and police patrol driver Charley Houser.[1]

Later, the county court, in a compromise between its legal restrictions and compassion, allowed claims from the three mortuaries for one-half the expenses of the burials: "Ollie Crosswhite, $125.00, Wiley M. Mashburn $154.69, Albert S. Meadows, $119.25."[2]

Dr. Stone ordered all the bodies removed to the Alma

Lohmeyer Funeral Home for autopsies. A reporter described that scene: "All six bodies were laid in a line on stretchers in a large parlor pending the arrival of the coroner. Each was covered with a sheet, and each sheet was stained red in several places."[3]

Several hundred persons soon materialized, all wanting to crowd into the funeral home. Finally the pressure of the mass of people became so great that "it was thought best to allow all who wished to file through the room where the shooting victims lay. The white shrouds were turned back, revealing to all who passed the blood-smeared faces of the officers whose daring had cost them their lives." Coroner Stone made a brief examination and released the bodies to relatives.[4]

In a bizarre coincidence characteristic of the entire saga of the massacre, at the exact hour of the first funerals in Springfield, Harry and Jennings were dying in the shootout in Houston. Also, during the hours of the afternoon funerals, Willie Florence Young, being interviewed yet again, sobbed out directions for the burial of her errant sons.

The first ceremony, "a brief funeral service," honored Ollie Crosswhite. It was held at eleven o'clock on Monday, at the W. L. Starne Mortuary on Walnut Street, one block from the police station. That funeral was followed by another service for Crosswhite in the afternoon at the Walnut Grove Methodist Church and burial in his birthplace, Brighton. The newspaper headlined: "Sorrowing Throng Pays Tribute to Crosswhite." Four hundred people crowded the mortuary with a "multitude of flowers and wreaths." The Reverend J. A. Sherman of the Walnut Grove Baptist Church delivered the eulogy. Reverend Sherman, "a white-haired, kindly-faced minister," had known Ollie all his life and lauded his "valiant way, always standing between danger and us. He gave his life to protect our homes."[5]

At two o'clock the second funeral, Wiley Mashburn's, was conducted in the Alma Lohmeyer Funeral Home. Evangelist J. A. Killian delivered the memorial. Despite a chilling rain,

"almost 500 friends, relatives and sympathetic Springfield-
ians gathered for the service." The active pallbearers were
Will Webb, county juvenile officer (once sheriff himself);
county juvenile officer W. K. (Kirthy) Webb (Will's son); deputy sheriffs Ernest Hodge and Ed Smith; Albert McCullogh;
Sam Trimble (a prominent banker); Sam Herrick; and Albert
Bischoff (Sheriff Hendrix's brother-in-law). Nolen Burloch, a
Springfield Press reporter, said of Wiley's police escorts: "They
were Veterans who had fought danger many times with
Mashburn, regarded as one of the bravest peace officers
here."[6]

Tony Oliver's memorial, the third that day, took place at the
Grant Avenue Baptist Church, with burial in the Hazelwood
Cemetery in Springfield. The pallbearers, as in all the police
officers' services, were his fellow officers. They included
Frank Pike and Owen Brown. There was a long procession of
automobiles; it was said that "600 people crowded the small
church banked with flowers." The two songs were "Jesus
Savior Pilot Me" and "Rock of Ages." The newspapers
quoted at length from the sermon of the Reverend Thomas
H. Wiles. His theme in praise of detective chief Tony Oliver's
career was "Render therefore to all their due, tribute to
whom tribute is due—honor to whom honor" (Rom. 39:7).[7]

On Tuesday a slight conflict in hours delayed the Sid
Meadows service until 2:45 at the Fox Funeral Home. Nevertheless, "hundreds of citizens gathered to pay last tribute." The Reverend T. H. Wiles of the Grant Avenue Baptist
Church delivered the eulogy. "A motorcycle squad escorted
the body to the cemetery [Eastlawn]. Sergeant Chester
Brumley and Harrison Pearson led and the rear escort was
composed of Motorcycle Officers Tommy Fielder and Lester
Scott. Fellow workers of City Detective Sid Meadows
escorted him to his grave."[8]

Partly because of rank (his was the highest office among
the men killed), but also because of his widespread personal
popularity, more attention was paid martyred Sheriff Marcell Hendrix than the others. He lay in state at the American

Legion Home on Benton Avenue, and John H. Chapman reported, "More than 5000 view body of beloved peace officer." His funeral service, "perhaps the largest ever held in Springfield," was conducted by the Reverend Lewis M. Hale of the First Baptist Church. For the first and only time in their histories, the three competing newspapers carried identical information, quoting at length from the memorial services of all six officers. The service for Sheriff Hendrix, typically, began with the song "Life's Railroad" by R. D. Patterson of the Grant Avenue Baptist Church. The Reverend J. A. Wilson read the scripture: "Set your affection on things above, not things on the earth. For ye are dead and your life is hid with Christ in God" (Coloss. 3:3). A male quartet sang "Home of the Soul." Reverend Hale's sermon eulogized Sheriff Hendrix from the text, "For whosoever shall lose his life for my sake shall find it" (Matt. 16:21). He closed the service with Tennyson's "Crossing the Bar." Chapman's story concluded: "On a sequestered slope in Eastlawn Cemetery here last night slept Greene County's beloved Sheriff Marcell Hendrix."[9]

Because of the "collapse" of his wife, Charley Houser's service was delayed until Wednesday, the sixth. Dr. Lewis M. Hale officiated, and the text for his sermon, appropriately, was I Corinthians 13. A cortege of fellow police officers led by Chief Ed Waddle escorted the hearse to Joplin, and the Reverend Cliff Titus (soon to be one of the two Republicans in the thirty-four-body Missouri Senate) eulogized Charley Houser. He was buried in a family plot in the Fairview Cemetery at Joplin, where Harry and Jennings Young, too, were to be buried.[10]

Other church groups gave memorial ceremonies. The Greene County Baptist ministers "extended their sympathies" to the bereaved wives and families. The Ash Grove Baptist Church, "filled to capacity," paid tribute to the six slain officers.[11] In addition to the individual pastoral services for each of the officers, there was an unusual ceremony on Sunday in which the Protestant ministers of the city memorialized all the officers. On Monday the *Springfield Daily News* headlined: "Agitated Congregations Join Ministers in Prayers for Officers." The concluding testimonial of the Reverend J. Crowell of the Woodland Heights Presbyterian Church was typical: "They substituted for us in the enforcement of law even as Christ showed willingness to be substituted for our sins."[12]

In Springfield, Eastlawn Cemetery offered burial plots for all the slain officers; two families, those of Sid Meadows and Wiley Mashburn, accepted these gifts.

PUBLIC TRIBUTES—DECLARATIONS

Many civic organizations passed resolutions praising the courage and dedication of the deceased officers and offering sympathy and condolence to their families. On Tuesday the press reported the resolve of the Rotary Club of Springfield: "Enterprises of concern and moment must pause while we pay tribute and respect to our brave officers of the law."[13]

The high point was a public memorial service in which state, county, and city joined to "voice the appreciation . . . for the valiant manner in which the men died." A "joint funeral [for the six] was found impracticable," so the Goad-Ballinger Post of the American Legion sponsored the mammoth tribute, with W. R. Awbrey (a lawyer and veteran of World War I) as chairman. The Reverend G. Bryant Drake, a Congregational minister, was "in charge of devotionals." Officials of all ranks, along with ministers and other dignitaries, occupied the stage of the Landers Theatre at 2:30 Sunday. The theater had a 1,500-seat capacity. The crowd overflowed into Walnut Street. Governor Henry S. Caulfield, escorted by Arthur M. Curtis (state chairman of the Republican party), occupied the center of the crowded stage.[14]

Both Dan M. Nee, the prosecuting attorney, and Edward M. Barbour, Jr., the city attorney, knew all the officers well. In their official capacities they had become intimately acquainted with every member of the sheriff's staff and every member of the police force. The two were called upon to eulogize the men publicly. Dan Nee said, "These men worshipped the performance of duty as their mistress. They served faithfully, loyally, and honorably for our city and Greene County." Senator Ed Barbour, known to his dead friends as a down-to-earth fellow, was roused to stentorian eloquence before the sobering throng in the Landers Theatre:

"All our heroes have not died on the field of battle. The unknown soldier who sleeps on the slopes of Arlington yonder was no greater than these men sworn to uphold the law, they did not go out to the tune of fife and drum, but they were among the ranks of those whose relentless master was duty, and they did their duty. Death has not made heroes of these men. Death has not endowed them with attributes of honesty and integrity which they did not already have. Let us remember these men as they were alive and revere their memory. What a heroic image they have left to their loved ones. We are not selfish when we ask to share this inheritance with them."[15]

Strangely, in all the services, tributes, resolutions and memorials, it did not occur to anyone to mention that the event they were immortalizing was the killing of the largest number of law enforcement officers who were attempting a simple arrest. In all the declarations of gratitude, no one publicly called attention to the magnitude and horror of the catastrophe nor mentioned that their subjects were unnecessary victims of the largest massacre of police officers in the history of the nation. The obvious lesson to be learned was entirely neglected—the need for scientific, intelligent training of those charged with law enforcement, including instruction in the capture and arrest of criminals. The one small nod in this direction was on Tuesday, the day the Young brothers died; Mayor Gideon did take the opportunity to recommend the purchase of "high-powered rifles" for the protection of the city police force.

POETRY

On Sunday morning, January 10, the *Sunday News and Leader* published a day-by-day, hour-by-hour recapitulation, headlined, "Full Graphic History of Massacre at Young Farm." A subhead declared that it had been the "Most Frightful Week in Springfield's History Since Civil War. Fixed Accurately as Possible from Hurried Stories."

The dramatic account of these momentous events had inspired a prodigious spate of verse from all over southwest Missouri. In addition to its condensed history of the massacre, the Sunday paper printed a selection of those outpourings: "Poems in Praise of Slain Officers' Heroism." The inspired poets lived in Arno, Taneycomo, Bolivar, and Seligman, as well as Springfield. A few titles were "Will We Remember?," "A Tribute to Six Brave Men," "Requiem for Our Slain Heroes," "Departing in Peace Or In Terror." Typical was Elmo Ingenthron's poem, "The Sickles Cut Them Down." The poem concludes: "Yet the flower of life was taken away / But the thistles cannot thrive / For the flower does as those brave men / Leaving the seed of hope, courage and honor / To the thousands of mourning lives / Even though the sickles cut them down."[16]

COUNTERPOINT

As these lofty words were written, some sour notes were heard. Pointed questions, warnings, analyses, and inquiries abounded. "What's wrong in the Ozarks?" several newspapers asked portentously. Jake Fleagle had recently been killed when law enforcement officers entrapped him in a railroad passenger car near Branson. "Pretty Boy" Floyd had been through southwest Missouri frequently. Missouri State Highway Patrol officers had searched a motel room on Lake Taneycomo only a few hours after Floyd and his gang had hurriedly departed, leaving gang photographs behind. Others reported the presence of numerous criminals in the Ozarks, including the Oglesby gang and the Barkers. Police officer Ben Bilyeu fired the flame of speculation when he "identified a picture of Barker as a man glimpsed [by him] in the [Young] death house." At the inquest he testified that "Barker appeared at a lower window. I tried to shoot but my gun clicked harmlessly and I dashed back to the car." The *St. Joseph News Press* said, "The sobering fact seems to be that the law has not caught up with the professional and methodical criminal."[17]

The august *St. Louis Post-Dispatch* was one of the papers posing the rhetorical question: "What's wrong with the Ozarks?" Its editorial answer, unmindful of crime in St. Louis, was, "The country is admittedly an inviting retreat for desperadoes wanted by the law. That is what is wrong down there. It offers attractive opportunity for the basic industry of the professional criminal class, namely the illicit liquor traffic. It is too bad."

Even as a small city in those days, and in the days of extensive lead mining, Joplin was not noted for its piety and reverence for law observance. Nevertheless, the *Joplin Globe* lectured: "There is pity, of course, for the 66-year-old mother of the Youngs. While she must have been in part responsible for their poor bringing up, it is easy to go farther back and say someone else was responsible for the insufficient training of a woman who could become a mother with such inadequacy." The *St. Louis Star* said: "The six officers who lost their lives were brave men, recklessly brave. The killing was an outbreak of lawlessness remindful of the worst days of the Bald Knobbers [no law-enforcement officers were killed or involved in those 1886 episodes] in the same neighborhood, and the James and Quantril gangs."[18]

BURIALS

There is a fine line between a full-fledged memorial or funeral and a mere burial. Willie Florence Young was aware of the distinction. Appropriately enough, funeral and memorial services were held for the dead officers; Harry and Jennings Young were unceremoniously buried.

When told that her sons were dead, Willie "prayed they'd do it. I prayed they would. I hope they took the time to ask

God to forgive them." She was interviewed and filmed for Movietone News, and Frank Wiley, the jailer, asked her during the filming if she thought there was any chance for her sons to be forgiven. She replied, "Oh, I don't know. I've been waiting for word down there to see if they said anything before they died. I don't know whether they could be forgiven or not. He said, though, 'Whatever you ask, you shall receive.'"[19]

Her daughters Gladys and Mary Ellen arrived, as well as a son-in-law and an infant grandchild. Florence, soon to arrive and take charge, was directing affairs in Houston. A reporter for the *Daily News* wrote that Gladys and Mary Ellen tried to reassure their distraught mother, saying, "You have the rest of us to live for—and we won't give you any trouble."

Soon, Mom's attention was necessarily focused on the burial of her sons. In the presence of reporter Lucile Morris Upton, Frank Wiley asked where she wanted her sons to be buried. "I want them buried beside their father in the McCauley Cemetery [near Ozark]. And I want to go and I want to see them."

Willie had visions of an appropriate funeral ceremony "with a brief prayer." She envisioned Dr. Lewis M. Hale "giving a good prayer" and someone to sing "Rock of Ages," a song she said "Harry constantly sang when he 'went crazy' about 12 years ago." She had in mind a talented lady friend "to make a nice spray of flowers." She said, "I want to get out of here and go to the cemetery and I want the girls to go." It goes without saying that these dreams did not materialize.[20]

Confusion, interference, and indecision reigned. No one seemed to know what, officially, should be done with the bodies of the Young brothers. Ugly rumors surfaced of plans to mutilate them (a rumor that Florence tried to hide from her mother).

Florence telephoned and was permitted to tell a "weepingly protesting mother" that it would be best, as their wives had requested, that "the boys" be buried in Houston. She comforted her mother: "Now, Mother, don't worry. You couldn't help it. You just be brave." Mom lamented: "Poor Florence, poor Florence. She and Paul [then sought by the Houston police] are the only ones down there. It will be terrible for them. Poor Vinita. She is over there in an awful condition. Oh, my poor children!"[21]

Before any burial plans were firmly made, the question of reward arose. Some officials insisted that the bodies had to be returned to allow "dead or alive" identification.

Meanwhile, Mrs. Young gave mortician W. L. Starne written authority to return the bodies to Missouri, for burial in the McCauley Cemetery. A macabre journey then began. Armed with Willie's written authorization and a deputy sheriff's commission, Starne and his driver Rex Rainey sped to Houston.

After much discussion and the payment of fees, the bodies, "not boxed, merely embalmed and lying on cots," were released to Starne and his driver. The two set off, hurriedly, on a circuitous route through Louisiana and Oklahoma to Greene County. The newspaper headline was "Keep Young Bodies Hidden." The story reported, "At every town from Houston to Vinita [Oklahoma], traffic was all but blocked by spectators." When they arrived at Vinita, they were held up for two hours. Starne reported, "The wives of the boys overtook me, and when I told them Chief Waddle's wishes they instructed me to leave the bodies behind and not return them until further notified." In desperation, he promised the women not to tell where the bodies were stored, and he was permitted to go to Pittsburg, Kansas, where the bodies stayed the night in Gee's Undertaking Parlor.[22]

Meanwhile, prosecutor Nee telephoned Sheriff Harry D. Stephens "to hold the bodies in Carthage [Missouri] until this morning [Wednesday]." At the Greene County-Lawrence County line a large crowd led by police officers intercepted the cortege. Starne was stopped. Officer Tommy Fielder identified the bodies. The hearse turned back to Joplin. There, Harry and Jennings Young were buried, in the Fairview Cemetery.[23]

In almost a parody of Mom's dream of an appropriate funeral, a "secretive group of about 50 persons" and "fifteen kinsmen gathered beside the two open graves." The dead men's wives were not present. Among the officials attending were prosecutor Nee and his assistant, Jim Hornbostel, along with Lee Jones and Owen Brown. Vinita and Lorena, handcuffed together, and Albert, Oscar, and Willie were accompanied by their jailers. The service was described as "brief, grim, almost furtive." No minister from any church was there. Over Starne's vigorous protests the ceremony was interrupted, and the caskets were opened yet again, to allow another official identification and fingerprinting, this time by private detective Linker.

Beth Campbell described the ceremony: "Two gray velour coffins" were lifted from the hearse. On a panel atop the caskets were inscribed the words "At Rest." Mrs. Young, "in a black suede coat and black felt hat with bands of green and orange, a necklace of gold and cornelian beads, and a figured white scarf pinned about her throat led the family." The well-dressed sisters "seemed chiefly concerned with their mother." Mom, supported by her daughters, circled each casket, "sobbing and groaning," uttering prayers for forgiveness. She fainted once. Undertaker W. L. Starne "mumbled a brief ritual," from which Campbell quoted: "The Lord giveth and the Lord taketh away." And, "in a monotone," he closed, "looking forward to the resurrection and the coming of the Saviour who will redeem all sin." Six volunteers, employees of the city cemetery, acted as bearers and, on a signal from Starne, lowered the caskets into the side-by-side graves. A footstone, provided by Vinita in later years, marks the site. To this day it is visited now and then by the curious.

Willie and Oscar were returned to the Greene County Jail by deputy sheriff Hodge. The other women and Albert were taken to the Springfield City Jail by grocery salesman Bryan Van Hook, escorted by motorcycle officers Lester Scott and Chet Brumley. A janitor provided the daughters with a sponge, warm water, and soap, "and they scrubbed the joint cell to the brightness of new money."[24]

On the day Harry and Jennings died, the widows of the slain policemen, victims themselves in every sense, were interviewed. Mrs. Hendrix sat in the room "where the body of the slain Sheriff lay," opening cards of sympathy and flowers. "He loved red roses so," she said. Maud Hendrix responded to the news that the Young brothers were killed: "I'm glad—But that won't bring Marcell back." Mrs. Oliver (also Maud) said, "I haven't much to say and I'm not bitter toward no one, for bitterness cannot correct this terrible affair. Wanted the killers brought to justice, though. What I wish to say more than anything else is something about our thanks to the many wonderful friends for their kindness and the sympathy shown us in the darkest hour of our lives." Ethel Crosswhite was emotionally exhausted, prostrate. Augusta Houser was ill. They were not available for comment on the death of the Young brothers. Lillie Meadows was in no beatific mood; her bitterness came out emphatically: "I'm glad the whole thing is over! I'm sorry that they were not taken alive. I wanted them brought back here and hanged."[25]

NOBLE BENEFACTORS

On Sunday a front-page editorial praised the six men "who died gallantly, a hero to everyone, in defense of you, your property and your homes." Opposite the editorial a news story detailed the meager resources and small estates left by the officers. Except for their own strong inner resources, five of the widows and their families were all but destitute. Only Sheriff Hendrix, a successful farm operator, was deemed affluent in the days of the Great Depression. The editorial concluded, "They have left behind sorrowing widows and little children," and "it is now our duty to do our duty nobly as they did theirs." The news article urged "a fund to be shared as their needs require, by their survivors to lessen their sorrows and their burdens as much as material aid can lighten them."[26]

Sophisticated fund-raisers, with computers and the entic-
ing money-raising ploys of the 1980s, were unknown in 1932.
All that was available to a sorrowing community was what
social workers would later call "mutual aid." In the beginning
a loosely formed, all-but-leaderless "Benefit Fund" was proposed. Arch McGregor, a highly respected and successful
hardware merchant, volunteered an unprecedented $1,000. A
large group of the city's successful citizens gathered to discuss
the situation. Questions arose as to who would administer the
fund. "Mr. Arch" was unanimously proposed, and he
promptly replied, "By George, I'll accept."

Immediately, the *Springfield Leader* headlined: "Leaders of
Civic, Professional and Business Groups Joined Forces: Volunteers Pledge Near $3,000." Even before the funerals,
members of the Springfield Chamber of Commerce had per-
fected an organization to lead a drive for funds. Nineteen
committees, representing every phase of life in Springfield,
were appointed, each chaired by a recognized leader. The
committees represented civic clubs, educational institutions, merchants at all levels, lawyers, doctors, fraternal
organizations, women's clubs, and public utilities, all by
name. A twentieth group was a five-man committee to
administer the fund: Arch McGregor, chairman, C. O.
Sperry (a successful northside real estate developer), Dan
Nee, Louis Barth (owner of a men's clothing store), and Wal-
ter Eisenmeyer (owner of a flour mill). E. C. Smith, the
respected secretary of the Chamber of Commerce, was
assigned the task of receiving the contributions.

There were daily reports of gatherings. Pleas were sent
out: "No gift too small, no gift too big for usefulness." Each
morning and evening the newspapers printed the names of
volunteers and donors. The amounts of contributions
ranged from one to one hundred dollars. McGregor's $1,000
was to remain the largest single gift. On January 8 the Union
National Bank made the next largest pledge—$500. The fire
department "generously gave $67," and the fund "For
Dependent Families of Slain Officers Passes $5,000 Mark."[27]

As early as Monday afternoon the sports section of the *Leader* headlined: "Benefit Boxing Card for Slain Officers' Families." Leonard Short was the promoter. (Leonard was also known as the brother of famous Republican congressman Dewey Short, the "boy orator of the Ozarks.") The boxing match was to feature three preliminaries and a "twelve round fistic battle," Chuck Raines against Wilson Dunn. From that event "a percentage of the 30 round card" went to the subscription fund for the six officers. According to the *Springfield Daily News*, "There was a rematch of Raines against Dunn at the American Legion, admission tickets $1.50 and $1.00, with a goal of $300, 30% to the fund and 70% for expenses."[28]

The grand finale of these fund-raising events was a local talent Officers' Benefit Revue, sponsored jointly by the Springfield police and fire departments. Impresario Larry Blanchette staged, produced, and took part in the sixteen-act extravaganza, and local performers donated their services. Glen Stambach's popular band played, featuring, among others, the well-known Mickey Marcell. There were two quartets, one of which, "Close Harmony," consisted of Ira Smith, Ted Trapp, George Aldridge (all well-known singers), and "Boots" Miller, a one-armed police detective and son of the 1932 United States deputy marshal William Miller. "Boots" and his father were both at the Young farm on Saturday night after the massacre, and "Boots" is easily identifiable in several photographs of the throng. The Police String Quartet featured officers Ralph Sutter, Red Pierson, versatile Frank Pike (a maker of guitars), and "Goo-Goo" Rutledge. Rutledge had been a comedian-guitarist with the Weaver Brothers and Elviry, a local group who became nationally renowned hillbilly entertainers, even playing the Palace in New York long before Nashville's Grand Ole Opry. This revue added $732 to the "widow fund," raising the total amount to $9,455.[29]

The final total, as reported by John R. Woodside, exceeded eleven thousand dollars, "to be expended as, when and where needed among the beneficiaries."[30] There is no record of how the funds were finally disbursed and no accounting of the fund. The records of the Chamber of Commerce have vanished. In March 1985, Ray Oliver, who was fourteen years old when his father died, reported that his mother gratefully received $55 a month from the fund for three years.

Even this lofty venture yielded a bizarre incongruity. Steve McLaughlin officially recorded that Charley Houser was a "faithful, devoted and always cheerful husband." However, it was soon discovered that Charley and Augusta were cohabiting without ever having been married. The now-common practice of "live-in" mates was a totally unheard-of relationship in 1932, one that would not have been condoned even for the highest motives. It was concubinage, "living in sin," and could not be publicly recognized even for benevolent purposes. Thus, despite Charley's vaunted martyrdom and Augusta's distraught collapse, to quote Ray Oliver, "She never got a penny."[31]

REWARDS

The concept of reward has many aspects. The definition given in the *American Heritage Dictionary* (1979), "something given or received in recompense for worthy behavior," does not exactly cover money given for the capture of a criminal. The concept of reward as *bounty* carries with it an unfortunate connotation. In legal parlance, *reward* is an ancient and highly technical contractual concept; there must be an expressly delineated offer on one side and a precise acceptance, in compliance with the offer, on the other side. Legalisms aside, there remains the ethical question for a professional: may or should a public official, a policeman, a sheriff, or other officer charged with the duty of enforcing the law accept or claim a reward?

Excitement to the point of hysteria followed when a report of the wrecked Ford coupe at Streetman reached Springfield. The public clamored for the creation of a reward for apprehending the Young brothers. Mayor Gideon proposed to call a special meeting of the city council. He suggested "a large reward for the capture, dead or alive, and conviction of these criminals." At the first council meeting, city attorney Barbour advised the group that in no event could the city legally offer a reward. It was suggested that the county court (an administrative agency, not a court) "discuss" the subject; Judge Sam Moore, typically, was heartily in favor of a "good, adequate reward for the capture of the killers." J. B. Alsup, a prominent farmer and crier for the Federal District Court and, most impressively, "Marshall of the Nichols Anti-Horse Thief Association," appeared before the court and urged that a reward be posted. In a telephone conversation, Governor Henry S. Caulfield told Dan Nee that the state would pay a reward of $300 "for the conviction of the killers." The state statute then and now authorizes the governor, in the case of fleeing felons, to "offer a reward of not to exceed $300 for the apprehension and delivery to the proper sheriff or other designated officer."[32]

On Tuesday, the fourth day after the massacre, simultaneously with the funerals of the slain officers, the county court met and entered a long, formal order saying that the six named officers were "slain while in the performance of their duties by a band of murderers composed of Harry and Jennings Young and possibly others unknown to the court." "Now, therefore," it was recited, "the court doth order that a reward of $500 be made and offered and the same is hereby made and offered for the capture and return, dead or alive, to the Officers of Greene County, Missouri, at Springfield, Missouri, of each of the following persons upon their positive identifications Harry Young, Jennings Young and/or other persons who shall be convicted of or proved to the satisfaction of the court to be one of the band of murderers of Sheriff Hendrix and five other peace officers."[33]

The governing law then, and now, authorized county courts that were "satisfied that any felony had been committed" to "offer a standing reward of not exceeding five hundred dollars for the apprehension and arrest" of the felon.

There was, however, this proviso: "In no instance shall any reward, or any part thereof, be paid . . . until final conviction of the defendant."

Immediately, speculation arose about who might accept a reward and how. Without reference to the governing laws, there was quibbling as to the meaning of terms, even of words in the offer, of "identification," and "return of bodies dead or alive" or "to the satisfaction of the court." Rumors spread that the bodies might be surreptitiously removed from their caskets and buried in Texas, as Florence wished. In that event, there could not be "positive identification" or "capture and return to Greene County dead or alive." Even Governor Caulfield, lawyer-like, expressed doubt that the reward could "legally" be paid unless the bodies were actually returned to Greene County. Deputy sheriff Hodge insisted on identification even though, in the morgue in Texas, "federal authorities fingerprinted the dead men and say the identification is positive." The *Houston Post-Dispatch* reported the position of the Greene County Court; quoting the Associated Press, however, the paper said that the court had recanted but would "observe the moral obligation and pay the rewards."[34]

Who, then, of all the people involved in bringing the Young brothers' ill-starred careers to an end, should share the reward, and who would finally determine the amount of the rewards? Only the judges of the County Court could finally determine to whom the reward would be paid. However, the court concluded, according to presiding Judge Young, that "they can only make recommendations" as to how the reward should be divided among multiple rewardees. Prosecutor Nee pointed out that A. E. Gaddy, Jr., had supplied the first tip that led to Houston. Another person mentioned his mother's "overhearing" Mr. Carroll's telephone call to Corsicana. In addition to the Houston police, who were actually present when the slayers were killed, the *Springfield Leader* suggested that Mr. Carroll, the farmer who found the car and guns, was "deserving."

On January 14, after conducting the burials of the Young brothers, W. L. Starne, the undertaker, appeared before a session of the County Court and presented the first claim— $500 of the $1000 reward. Prosecutor Nee refused to commit himself as to the validity of the claim. The basis of Starne's demand was "that he was in custody of the bodies when they were brought into Greene County" and exhibited to the city officers who identified them. After some deliberation, the claim was denied.

Without exception, everyone involved in both Texas and Missouri recommended that the carpenter, B. F. Tomlinson, who owned the house where the Young brothers were killed, be a recipient of some part of the reward. It was he who had alerted the Houston police to the Young brothers' whereabouts. Chief Heard said, "If there's any reward paid, Tomlinson will get his share." As to the valorous members of the Houston police force, doughty Chief Heard was hopeful but skeptical; he preferred "to wait till we get it to decide on the cut to be made. Since a score or more [13] officers took part in the Walker Avenue raid, the money probably will go to the police department 'burial and benefit fund.'"[35]

Chief Heard's skepticism was well founded. If a reward from either the state or the county was ever paid, there is no official record of it, and no one has been able to unearth a newspaper account of anyone's receiving a reward "for the capture and return, dead or alive" of Harry Young or Jennings Young. The Houston Police Department became politicized in the late 1930s and 1940s, and one of Mayor Oscar Holcombe's reforms was abolishing the police "burial and benefit fund." The police fund has been succeeded by the One Hundred Club, a private organization composed of businessmen who collect funds from the private sector to compensate the families of officers killed in the line of duty. Danny Hair, the public information officer of the reformed and modern Houston Police Department, reports that in its "scanty" archives there is no record of a reward being paid into any fund in the 1930s.[36]

Perhaps the language of the court's own offer of a reward is its own best expositor. As the Houston department contended, and as Judge Overstreet judicially determined, Harry and Jennings killed one another. Thus it may be that since they were not taken "dead or alive" by anyone else's agency, no one was eligible for the reward. This is one of the intriguing questions about the Young brothers massacre that remains unanswered after more than fifty years.

The only certainty in this, one of the many bizarre aspects of the episode, is that the "listening" telephone operator, Mrs. Gaddy, the farmer, Mr. Carroll, the carpenter Tomlinson, or the ten or more valorous members of the Houston police department were not beneficiaries of the vaunted gratitude of Greene County for the final ending of the Young brothers' criminal careers. Why? Perhaps this is just another instance of the many questions about the massacre to which, in fact, there is no confident answer.

The beleaguered carpenter Tomlinson may naively have thought that after his two lodgers were killed and his home ransacked by souvenir collectors his life would automatically return to normal. If so, he was in for a surprise. On Thursday Tomlinson received this odd note: "Pick your grave, for I will get you. (Signed) Paul Young." Later he would decide that the threat was written by a crank or a practical joker. Police Chief Heard, however, was taking no chances. "Authorities announced that their search for Paul Young, brother of the desperadoes, would continue unabated."[37] Ten days before, Paul had been detained and charged "with driving an automobile with the wrong license plate." Chief detective Kirk Irwin said that he did not want him on that pending charge. Rather, he "just wanted to look at him." There were still rumors and a lurking suspicion that Paul had some connection with the massacre, and prosecutor Nee had asked the Houston police to interrogate him. The Springfield papers printed a report "by a man who knows him" that he had seen Paul on Highway 66 on Wednesday near the Republic turnoff and had talked to him. The unnamed man said Paul was driving an old-model Ford, that "he was under the influence of liquor," and that he said he was there "to meet the Starne ambulance." Chief Waddle refused to comment on this report.[38]

Detective chief Irwin nonetheless issued "a blanket order" based on that report to be on the lookout for a blue Ford sedan. A citywide search for Paul began.

On Thursday, the Tomlinson home on Walker Street was empty, and the Tomlinsons "could not be reached for a statement." Chief Heard refused to deny or affirm that the Tomlinsons had received a death threat or that they were being hidden by the police.

On Friday a front-page photograph of Paul appeared in the *Houston Chronicle*. Accompanied by his lawyer, Arthur Heidingsfelder, Paul, "having nothing to be afraid of," surrendered at the police station. He denied to Chief Heard that he had any connection with the massacre in Springfield or that he had seen his brothers since they returned to Houston on Monday. He said of his brothers, however, "that if he had he would have helped them in any way possible."

Paul's Houston address was the boarding house of Jessie B. Martin, 2410 LaBranch. Jessie said of Paul that "he stayed there on and off for two years." He was there on Monday and "ate supper there Saturday night." Paul Young was questioned throughout the day by detective chief Kirk Irwin, who finally decided that Paul had nothing to do with the massacre or with the flight of his brothers. He was, nevertheless, held in the Houston jail.[39]

On February 20, 1932, Paul and his mother, "Mrs. J. P. Young, alias Willie Young," were charged "with transporting a stolen automobile from Houston, Texas, to Springfield, Missouri." Mrs. Young, arrested at the home of her daughter Florence, was alleged to "have fled from Missouri to Texas." Mom was not prosecuted; the case was transferred to the Federal Court in Springfield. Paul entered a plea of guilty and was sentenced to four years' imprisonment in Leavenworth Penitentiary.[40]

In 1966 Carl F. Zarter, an administrative assistant at the
United States Penitentiary in Leavenworth, reported that
the records showed that Paul had been "assigned to the shoe
factory." Prison is one place where time does not fly, but Paul
had learned how to cope with and adjust to prison life. He
was never "reported for any violation of institutional rules"
and was discharged "by expiration of sentence" on January
28, 1935.[41]

Even this, his ninth or tenth incarceration, was not a convincing deterrent. Only four months and twenty-one days
after leaving Leavenworth, Paul was indicted for having
embarked on a different criminal enterprise: he did "feloniously, abstract, take, steal and carry away from and, out
of the United States mail at Medford, Oklahoma, with intent
to convert to his own use a large amount of mail," three
pouches, containing specifically described checks. Again,
caught red-handed, he pleaded guilty in Oklahoma City
before Judge Edgar S. Vaught and was sentenced to serve
three more years in Leavenworth.[42]

Paul may have been slow to learn and hard to persuade,
but his discharge on October 31, 1937, was his last. After fifty
years of rectitudinous living, Paul made his peace with the
law and society. His FBI rap sheet shows that in March 1942
his application to the commanding general, Services of Sup-
ply, United States Army, for a job as a "ship-fitter" was pro-
cessed.[43] In his portly, affluent nonagenarianism his most
pressing fear and concern was the safety and security of his
lawfully accumulated money and property. He had invested
in expensive real estate "that nobody can run off with."

NEWS COVERAGE AND ANNIVERSARIES
Even in the depths of the Great Depression, Springfield
boasted three newspapers, all locally owned and locally
financed. Competition was fierce. All three—the *Springfield
Leader,* the *Springfield Press,* and the *Springfield Daily News*—
claimed to be first with all news of the massacre.

Such a monstrous and dramatic event would have evoked

full coverage in any case, but the striving of the financially pressed newspapers and their poorly paid reporters produced "blanket" coverage indeed. There were daily extras, and not a tiny event was left unremarked. The most intimate details of personal lives were examined and exposed. Every rumor was printed. The tragedy was thoroughly and completely revealed to the public, to the point of saturation. On Tuesday, for example, the *Press* boasted being the first by twenty-five minutes to print the news of the "suicide pact" and death of Harry and Jennings.[44] Headlines of the latest massacre news pushed aside the Democrats' annual Jackson Day, a momentous event in an election year. They obscured the death of Julius Rosenwald, whose influence in southwest Missouri had been great. Even the depression news of farm and financial woes was reduced to the obscurity of back pages.

The massacre, in all its fascinating aspects, was of much more than mere local interest. The killing of the largest number of law enforcement officers in the history of the country, and the details of the pursuit and death of their assassins, made national front-page headline news for days.

Houston had two leading newspapers at the time: the *Houston Chronicle* and the *Houston Post-Dispatch*. The competition there, as in Springfield, was severe. When the Young brothers fled to Texas, their exploits overshadowed news of President Hoover, Gandhi, Raskob, Democratic politics, and controversies over legalizing alcoholic beverages. There was excellent complete newspaper coverage of the role of the Houston police and the pursuit and death of Harry and Jennings Young.

In a few weeks, Springfield Publishing Company, 308 E. McDaniel Street, issued a seventy-eight-page brochure with numerous photographs from the newspaper morgues, announcing itself as the "true account of America's Worst Peace Officer Massacre." The price was twenty-five cents. It purported, on its cover, to be "written and illustrated especially for law enforcement officers." It concluded with a

critique of the city of Springfield and the rout of its unfortunate law enforcement officers on January 2, 1932. The pamphlet was compiled and written "By John R. Woodside et al,"
and the flyleaf carries the notation "copyright 1932." Who
and what the Springfield Publishing Company may have
been no one knows. John R. Woodside was a respected
reporter. The "et al" were probably, among others, Erwin
Greenhaw, Frank Rhoades (*San Diego Union*), Max Boyd, and
Nolen Bulloch (*Tulsa World*), reporters for the three competing Springfield newspapers.

In July 1970, Woodside, speaking of the brochure, said,
"There was a police station buff who was always around
when I was police reporter for the old *Springfield Press*. For
the life of me I can't recall his name. He offered me $600 to
write a story of the so-called Massacre. We couldn't agree on
the treatment of the story, so I turned over my copy with the
understanding that he would pay me $300 for the use of my
name and the copy. I never did receive a penny."[45]

When asked about the copyright in August 1980, James C.
Roberts, head of the Reference Research Search Section of
the United States Copyright Office, officially confirmed that
"searches in the indexes and catalogs of the Copyright Office
covering the period 1898 through 1970 under names John R.
Woodside and Springfield Publishing Company, Missouri,
and the title (where available) THE YOUNG BROTHERS
MASSACRE, failed to disclose any separate registration for a
work identified under these names and this specific title."[46]

The Ralph Foster Museum, an integral section of the
School of the Ozarks at Point Lookout in Taney County, is an
unusual part of an unusual educational institution. The
museum, in the center of the campus, houses a collection of
collections: of automobiles, bugs, birds, coins, artifacts, and
folklore. Among these is a large glass case with the caption:
"America's Most Heinous Peace Officer Massacre." In it are
the guns, the handcuffs, and photographs of the slain
officers. It also displays composite photographs of pages
from the Springfield newspapers, a photograph of the

Woodside brochure, a photograph of the Young brothers, and, in all of this, the leggy poses of Vinita and Lorena.

Every anniversary of the massacre was the occasion for a story or sketch, especially by "Celia," Lucile Morris Upton, who wrote columns about the "good old days" in the persona of a mythical niece. Typical was one published as late as January 17, 1982: "Dearest Auntie: Shock and sorrow at the loss of our six law officers on January 2 has abated very little." She listed the names of the officers, concluding: "Our newspapers last week were calling it the 'Young Massacre' and one said the week following it had been the most frightful for Springfield since the Civil War."

On the tenth anniversary of the event, Friday, January 2, 1942, the *Springfield Leader Press* carried a brief resume with pictures of the farmhouse and Frank Pike in uniform pointing to the mounted pictures of his dead comrades.[47]

In July 1944, the *Chicago Herald American* ran a series of articles contending that "hunches" played a "big role" in the solution of murders. The paper claimed that police often "stopped cold [and] it remained to newspapermen, trained to follow hunches, to break the case." The 105th of Edgar Brown's "graphic series" demonstrated the point with the "Case of the Ozark Outlaws." A Houston copyreader, "nursing the granddaddy of hangovers" and reading a news item, "muttered two names." Those two names ignited his "hunch," which he says "trapped a pair of ruthless killers." The item that triggered his hunch was from the press report of Harry Young's murder of Mark Noe in 1929. The editor and copyreader printed a photograph of Harry Young which, in turn, led to Mr. Tomlinson's identification of his roomer. In rounding out his "graphic" series, Brown, in flamboyant prose, embellished the facts as related by Owen Brown, Frank Pike, and Chief Heard.[48]

For some years in the 1950s, George Olds published a monthly magazine called *Bias*. It was peevishly competitive and irksome to his former employers, the daily papers. On December 26, 1951, anticipating the twentieth anniversary of the massacre, *Bias* published a "two-chapter story of that ghastly deed, much of it based on that magazine, 'The Young Brothers,' by Duane Yarnell."[49] That interview and subsequent ones with Frank Pike evolved into the articles by Yarnell in *Men* magazine in 1955 and *Amazing Detective* in 1957.

On the fortieth anniversary, the *Sunday News and Leader* published staff writer Frank Farmer's extensive recreation of the Young massacre. The story included an interview with Frank Pike, the lone survivor, in which he remembered vividly "that dreary January 40 years ago." This time the emphasis, as one headline put it, was on "The Facts Behind the Legend of the Tragic 'Young Massacre.'" Another headline read: "How to Make a Legend Come Alive Again."[50]

On Sunday, January 3, 1982, the *News and Leader* printed a story by Renee Turner, captioned, "Fifty Years Later, Memory of Massacre Lives on." Ms. Turner observed that "a half century ago life was quite different in the Ozarks." It was, she said, "a time of great poverty." Citing the usual list— "Pretty Boy" Floyd, Dillinger, and the Barkers—she reported, "It was an era of bank robbers and holdups and sawed-off shotguns." For the facts of the massacre and its denouement, she quoted Mickey Brown, Owen's successful son. Here, for the first time, a news reporter sought a motivating factor that might have impelled the Young brothers toward a life of criminal activity. The concept of sociopathic career criminals was not widely accepted in 1932, nor, perhaps, was Ms. Turner familiar with it. She described the underlying factor in the criminality of the Young brothers as she saw it: "The Great Depression had turned many an honest man to a life of crime to feed his family." She quoted Mickey Brown: "Everybody was poor." Others, she said, "turned to crime for quite different reasons. Their lawlessness was spawned by the knowledge that they would become billboard heroes." She attributed the latter motivation to the Young brothers.[51]

A more pragmatic explanation may lie in two characteristics of the Young brothers that were known to their acquaintances: their inordinate, unfounded false pride, a flaw often observed in their youth; and the fact, observed by neighbors throughout their lives, that, as Robert Frost said, they "had a principled objection to work and the ingenuity to dodge it."[52]

There is also an undeniable thrill in living dangerously. Harry and Jennings were not deft or clever enough for "fast-buck" operations and, in defiance of the laws of probability, they resorted to the more elemental stratagems of burglary and automobile theft, at which they became adroit and fairly successful. After a brief review of their careers, however, Ms. Turner characterized the Young brothers as "gun-toting wise guys" and quoted an anonymous prison guard hearing Harry say, on his departure from prison: "You'll never get me inside again. Never. Not for anything."

With the fiftieth anniversary notice, the newspaper published one of the 1932 poems with a photograph of its author, Harry Wilson, then eighty-three years old. "The young brothers massacre" was a rhymed account of the two shoot-outs, ending with the tribute to men "Brave as brave men go" that Missouri "could number among her sons these brave and gallant men."[53]

"Celia," the surviving knowledgeable news reporter of the era, no longer writes "Dearest Auntie" about the "good old days." Thus, the anniversaries of the young brothers massacre have been neglected for several years.

Despite all the publicity, descendants of Willie Young are, for the most part, unaware of this historic episode in national criminality. They include grandchildren and scores of great-grandchildren. On the rare occasions when they meet, not ever again as a family group, the three surviving sisters, now all sedate ladies in their eighties, never mention the events of January 1932. To quote Vinita: "It is something you want to forget. I don't want to open that all up, it breaks your heart to even think of the past."

OMEGA

After the burials in Joplin, her mother and sisters in jail, her brother Oscar and wife on bond, the farm and its finances in shambles, Florence undertook to unravel Mom's overwhelming problems. At the burials, it was said, "she appeared in a black coat with karakul trim and black hat and looked extremely well." Florence was, in fact, as were her sisters, an attractive woman. The farm was sold, mortgages were satisfied, and all lawyers' fees, court costs, and debts were paid in full.

Willie and her possessions were installed in a house on South Street. She kept a few boarders, baby-sat for neighbors, and gradually adjusted to a new routine. The inherent strengths of mind and body that enabled her to homestead 160 acres of hard-scrabble land with J. D. and mother eleven children gradually restored tranquility and gave her the fortitude to face the world with grace and composure. Willie Florence Young died August 5, 1945, at age seventy-eight. She was buried in the McCauley Cemetery, in Ozark, next to "Daddy." Every Memorial Day for forty years, Vinita has traveled to the cemetery where, with tools and flowers, she carefully tends and decorates the family plot. "I don't cry and weep—I just think how wonderful and beautiful she was."

EPILOGUE

In pursuing desperate fugitives, hundreds of courageous law enforcement officers risk their lives daily, yet they are seldom heralded as heroes. In the saga of the young brothers massacre there were few heroes, only martyrs and disconcerted police officers. Fortunately, except for an occasional cumbersome contraband machine gun, there were then few of the rapid-firing hand guns, MAC11s, Ar-7s, and HK91s with the silencers that are now in the hands of many a berserk malefactor. More than fifty years would pass before dreadful events would erupt to challenge the Young brothers' record.

On October 4, 1985, eleven FBI agents converged on a Phoenix apartment to arrest a fugitive. "Special agent Robin Ahrens, 33, was killed by shots mistakenly fired by other agents," and, unfortunately, said the *New York Times*, she was "the first woman agent killed in the line of duty." Six months later, one agent was dismissed, one resigned, and three were disciplined. The fugitive was captured uninjured.[1]

On Friday, April 12, 1986, at 9:30 A.M., in the quiet Kendall residential area of Miami, the FBI achieved a new high point in ignominious defeat and humiliation. On that day a "task force" of eight experienced agents in four automobiles pursued two gunmen in a stolen black Monte Carlo bearing an identified stolen license plate. The two gunmen in the Monte Carlo were suspected of having committed six or more vicious, fatal bank robberies within the year. Joseph B. Corliss, the agent in charge of the Miami office, said that the gunmen, realizing that they were being followed, "slammed the car into a tree and came out firing an automatic weapon

(30 rounds a container) and a shotgun modified to hold more shells." FBI agents Benjamin T. Grogan and Donald Dove were killed instantly. In the ensuing ten-minute gun battle, hundreds of rounds were fired, and five agents armed with handguns and one shotgun were wounded. The wounded agents were Gorden McNeill, John Hanlon, Edmund Mirales, Richard Mannauzzi, and Gilbert Orrantia. The fleeing gunmen were William Matix, thirty-four, and Michael L. Platt, thirty-two, both dressed in army fatigues. Florida neighbors described Matix as a "born-again Christian who liked to give testimony in church to the memory of his dead wife" (whose life had been insured for $350,000) who, according to Columbus, Ohio, police may have been killed by Platt. One agent miraculously escaped the fusillade unharmed. Mirales, badly wounded in the left arm, "crawled about 20 feet, stood up, and shot the two suspects as they attempted to get away in a government car," the only vehicle not disabled, the Associated Press reported. According to *New York Times* reporter Jon Nordheimer, "a transcript of FBI radio transmission in the minutes leading up to the shootout indicated that the agents who were trailing the suspects thought the pair was planning to stage a holdup. The agents debated whether to wait or try to set a trap to arrest the pair before they could begin a holdup."[2]

FBI director William Webster described the shootout as an "incident," not a "massacre," presumably since only two people died and five were wounded. The April 21, 1986, issue of *Time* magazine mentioned this historic episode only incidentally in an article on the National Rifle Association's "powerful lobby [against all law enforcement organizations] push for lesser gun controls." The article concluded: "The casualties were the worst ever suffered by the FBI in a single incident."[3]

United States attorney general Edwin Meese, reacting to the episode, said, "This is a kind of thing that can happen. We're just glad these two men were stopped." Judge Webster responded to the suggested possibility of inadequate firepower: "This was a very good surveillance effort" by "brave and commendable agents" who "responded quickly and in a way to best protect innocent lives." When pressed by an Associated Press reporter about a "lack of matching fire power between his revolver-armed agents and semi-automatic weapons," the director replied that the agency "had no information that these guys had such high powered weapons." And, he concluded, "in robberies blamed on the two, they had used shotguns."[4]

In the hands of Harry and Jennings Young these lethal automatic weapons, "capable of firing at least 30 rounds in a single container," would have wiped out a regiment of law enforcement officers armed with conventional pistols and rifles.

NOTES

CHAPTER 1: HEARTBREAK FARMING IN OKLAHOMA

1. *A Diamond Jubilee History of Tillman County [Oklahoma], 1901–1976*, vol. 1 (Frederick, Okla.: Tillman County Historical Society, 1976), p. 712. Family photographs supplied by Vinita Young, March 17, 1979.

2. *A Diamond Jubilee History,* p. 7.

3. Ibid., pp. 91, 145, 712.

4. Report, Oklahoma Department of Agriculture-Statistics for Agriculture, pp. 13, 656–57, supplement, p. 640.

5. *A Diamond Jubilee History,* p. 145.

6. Vinita Young, conversation, March 17, 1979.

7. Howard M. McBee, private communication, August 3, 1981.

8. Records, vol. 82, p. 95, Office of Recorder of Deeds of Christian County (Missouri), March 2, 1918, June 2, 1918.

9. Office of the Circuit Clerk of Christian County (Missouri), cases 944, 945, 946, May 1918, January 23, 1919: *State* vs. *Paul Young and Jennings Young.*

10. Office of Recorder of Deeds, Greene County, Missouri, book 376, p. 478, warranty deed.

11. Priscilla and Edgar Miller, private communication, December 9, 1974.

12. Photographs and diagrams in John R. Woodside et al., "Young Brothers' Massacre," unpublished pamphlet, pp. 9, 23, 28, and 30, and numerous other photographs of Young house.

13. William Miller, conversation, March 28, 1972.

14. Priscilla and Edgar Miller, private communication, December 9, 1974.

CHAPTER 2: CRIMINAL CAREERS, COUNTRY STYLE

1. *Christian County Republican,* December 27, 1918—"A Republican paper published in the interests of Christian County."

2. Personal reminiscence, more than seventy years later.

3. Files, Christian County (Missouri) clerk.

4. *Christian County Republican,* December 27, 1918.

5. "Sentence and judgment of the court," Circuit Court of Christian County (Missouri), May 31, 1919.

6. Original records and photographs, Identifications and Records, Department of Corrections, Jefferson City, Missouri.

7. Ibid., and identification records in detail.

8. *Springfield Leader,* January 4, 1932.

9. Governor Arthur M. Hyde's commutation of sentence attested by Charles U. Becker, secretary of state, September 23, 1922.

CHAPTER 3: YOUNGS ACCUSED OF BOXCAR BURGLARY

1. Files, U. S. District Court, Western District of Missouri, A. L. Arnold, clerk, April 5, 1924, cases 3064–11 and 1317 ff.

2. Comer Owens, interview, August 11, 1979; Mickey Owens, interview, August 11, 1970.

3. Colonel Rufus Burrus, private communication, April 11, 1984.

4. Personal encounter with General Truman and report of incident by bartender, Colonial Lounge, 1950s, Springfield, Missouri.

5. *Congressional Record*, United States Senate, May 9, 1962, pp. 7470–71.

6. *Independence Examiner*, May 1, 1962; *New York Times*, May 1, 1962; *Kansas City Times*, editorial, May 2, 1962.

7. Files and records, U. S. District Court, Western District of Missouri, April 4, 1924.

8. Abstract of title to Young farm in Greene County, July 28, 1918–April 10, 1939.

9. Indictment, U.S. District Court, Western District of Missouri, September 7, 1924.

10. Files and records, U. S. District Court, Western District of Missouri, April 5, 1924.

11. *Official Manual State of Missouri* (Blue Book) 1929–1930, pp. 48–49, 1921–1922, p. 31.

12. Circuit Court of Greene County (Missouri), September term, 1932; *Fate Montgomery* vs. *Willie C. Young and Florence Mackey.* Order of publication in Commercial Events, August 15, 1932. Docket entry, circuit clerk, March 20, 1933, p. 255.

13. Abstract, title to Young farm, pp. 92–100.

CHAPTER 4: PAUL ON A CAREER PATH OF HIS OWN

1. Clerk, District Court, Bell County, Texas, January 24, 1924.

2. Texas State Penitentiary Records, "Description of Convict When Received," "Convict's Biography," April 6, 1924.

3. "Proclamation by the Governor of the State of Texas," signed "Miriam A. Ferguson, Governor of Texas," attested by secretary of state, February 21, 1925.

CHAPTER 5: A BUSY YEAR FOR HARRY

1. File, and record, Circuit Court, Greene County (Missouri), *State* vs. *Harry Young*, #8700, November 25, 1925.

2. *State* vs. *Harry Young*, #8706, March 28, 1927.

3. *State* vs. *Harry Young*, #8704, March 28, 1927.

4. *State* vs. *Harry Young*, #8707, March 28, 1927.

5. Missouri State Penitentiary, Reg. No. 31358, April 27, 1927. Original records available from Records Management and Archives Division, Office of Secretary of State, 1001 Industrial Drive, Jefferson City, MO 65101.

6. Freeman R. Bosley, Jr., circuit clerk, city of St. Louis, private communication, April 24, 1984. Record book, Criminal Court of St. Louis.

7. Record, Missouri State Penitentiary, Archives Division.

8. Vinita Young, conversations, January 21, 1982, October 25, 1982.

9. *State* vs. *Richette* (1938) 342 Mo 1015, l.c. 1026–29.

CHAPTER 6: HARRY SLAYS MARK S. NOE

1. *Republic Monitor,* June 6, 1929.

2. Ibid.; *Springfield News & Leader,* January 3, 1932; *Springfield Leader,* January 5, 1932; June 3–7, 1929.

3. *Republic Monitor,* June 6, 1929, quoting coroner Dr. Murray C. Stone.

4. Dorothy M. Dick, private communication, May 3, 1972, search of records with Judge Orville F. Kerr and deputy circuit court clerk.

5. *Cemeteries of Greene County,* vol. 3, by Cochran, Missouri Department of Archives.

6. Greene County Probate Court Records, file no. 8233, August 24, 1931, order refusing letters of administration.

7. *Republic Monitor,* June 6, 1929.

8. *Springfield Daily News,* January 5, 1932.

9. Ibid.

CHAPTER 7: JENNINGS IN JAIL AGAIN

1. District Court of the United States, Northern Judicial District of Texas at Ft. Worth, March 31, 1930.

2. Carl F. Zarter, administrative assistant, Classification to Parole, United States Penitentiary, Leavenworth, Kansas, private communication, September 30, 1966.

3. District Court of the United States, Northern Judicial District of Texas at Ft. Worth, March 31, 1930.

4. Thomas E. Gage and Gary R. Kremer, unpublished article, Missouri State Library; and "The Prison Problem in Missouri, A Survey: The Prison Industries Reorganization Administration," Missouri Supreme Court, Library Ref. 365.91, June 24, 1938, unpublished.

5. Question asked by Paul Barrett while on a tour of Missouri State Penitentiary, 1942, conducted by William "Boots" Miller, director, Department of Penal Institutions.

6. Ibid.

7. Kremer and Gage note one important instance when the deplorable

conditions in the Missouri penitentiary were brought to national attention, conditions that existed when Paul and Jennings served their sentences. In 1919, prison administrators began contracting to keep federal prisoners as well as the customary state inmates. Among them were the notorious Emma Goldman and Kate O'Hare, who had been convicted of espionage during the war. Their outpourings against conditions in the Missouri penitentiary were prolific. Sadly, little heed was paid these radicals.

CHAPTER 8: SPRINGFIELD'S FINEST— VICTIMS OF THE MASSACRE

1. Gideon's son, Oliver, also a lawyer, was father-in-law to television personality Bob Barker.

2. *Review, Police Department, Springfield, Missouri 1930*, (Springfield, Mo.: Springfield Press, 1930).

3. Tom Fielder, interview, July 27, 1970.

4. *Springfield Leader*, November 1931, photo and story of Marcell "chaw."

5. Ibid., January 3, 1982; Lucile Morris Upton (Celia), "Good Old Days."

6. Raymond Crosswhite, interview, March 12, 1985.

7. Ibid.

8. Frank Pike, interview, October 28, 1971.

9. Comer Owens, interview, August 11, 1970.

10. As assistant prosecuting attorney, Greene County, May 1929, extensive interview with Wiley Mashburn and Ollie Crosswhite.

11. *Springfield Press*, January 5, 1932.

12. McLaughlin, *Police Department 1930*, p. 10.

13. Frank Pike, interview, July 28, 1970.

14. Stephen McLaughlin, *Souvenir Review of Springfield Police Department* (Springfield, Mo.: Springfield Press, 1932), p. 24.

15. Letter, January 11, 1932, to Progressive Life Ins. Co., signed by Lillie B. Meadows. Copy of check for $1,000 to Lillie B. Meadows from Progressive Life Ins. Co., Rogers, Ark., dated January 9, 1932.

16. Lucile Thompson, interview, April 3, 1985; *Springfield Leader*, January 3, 1981.

17. McLaughlin, *Souvenir Review*.

18. *Springfield Leader*, February 1, 1981, Lucile Morris Upton, "Good Old Days."

19. McLaughlin, *Souvenir Review*.

CHAPTER 9: CLOUDS OF DISASTER GATHER

1. J. R. Woodside, et al., "Young Brothers' Massacre," unpublished pamphlet. Copies of photographs, pages 9, 23, 28, 30, and 34. Original

photographs were all destroyed in a fire at Springfield Newspapers in the late 1940s. Bill Southerland, editor, *Daily News, Springfield Leader & Press*, private communication, August 30, 1985.

2. Vinita Young, interview, April 21, 1981.

3. *Springfield Leader,* January 4, 1932.

4. Ibid., June 5, 1932; *St. Louis Post-Dispatch*, January 5, 1932.

5. *Houston Chronicle,* January 5, 1932.

6. *Springfield Leader,* January 4, 1932.

7. *Springfield Press,* January 4, 1932.

8. *Springfield Daily News,* January 4, 1932.

9. Ibid.

10. *Springfield Leader,* January 7, 1932.

11. Ibid., January 3, 1932.

12. Clyde Medley, private communication, April 28, 1985.

13. *Springfield Daily News,* January 3, 1932; *Springfield Leader,* January 3, 1932.

14. *Springfield Leader,* January 4, 1932.

15. *Springfield Daily News,* January 4, 1932; *Springfield Leader,* January 4, 1932.

16. *Springfield Press,* January 6, 1932; *St. Louis Post-Dispatch*, January 4, 1932.

CHAPTER 10: THE MASSACRE

1. Daily local record, Weather Bureau, U. S. Department of Agriculture, Springfield, Missouri, January 2, 1932.

2. Vinita Young, interview, January 21, 1982.

3. *St. Louis Post-Dispatch,* January 4, 1932.

4. *Springfield Daily News,* January 4, 1932.

5. *Springfield Leader,* January 3, 1932.

6. Vinita Young, conversation, November 4, 1984.

7. Stephen McLaughlin, "Who's Who of Greene County 1932," Springfield Police Department, 1932.

8. *St. Louis Post-Dispatch,* January 4, 1932.

9. *Springfield Leader,* January 4, 1932.

10. John R. Woodside, "Young Brothers' Massacre," unpublished pamphlet, p. 22. The history is a composite of the accounts in the three Springfield newspapers of January 3, 4, and 5, 1932.

11. *Springfield Press,* Extra, January 5, 1932; *Springfield Leader,* January 3, 1932.

12. *St. Louis Post-Dispatch,* January 4, 1932; *Springfield Leader,* January 5, 1932, report of inquest, testimony of survivors and others before coroner's jury. These reports were news across the nation in newspapers and on radio January 4 and 5, 1932.

13. Frank Pike, personal interview; Vinita Young, personal interview, April 21, 1981; *Springfield Leader,* January 3, 1932.

14. *Springfield Leader,* January 5, 1932.

15. Ibid.

16. Ibid.

17. Ibid., January 6 and 11, 1932.

18. *Springfield Press*, Extra, January 5, 1932.

19. *True Detective Magazine*, April 1932, pp. 15–20.

20. *Men*, December 1955.

21. *Springfield Leader*, January 3, 1932; *St. Louis Post-Dispatch*, January 4, 1932.

22. *Springfield Press*, Third Extra, January 5, 1932.

23. *St. Louis Post-Dispatch*, January 3, 1932.

24. *Springfield Leader*, January 5, 1932.

25. Ibid.; *Springfield Daily News*, January 6, 1932; *Springfield Press*, January 5 and 7, 1932.

26. *Springfield News and Leader*, January 3, 1932; *Springfield Leader*, January 5, 1932.

27. *Springfield Press*, January 6, 1932; *Springfield Leader*, January 3, 1932.

28. *Springfield Daily News*, January 4, 1932; *Springfield Leader*, January 3, 1932.

29. *Springfield Leader*, January 2, 1932.

30. *Springfield Leader*, January 4, 1932.

31. *Springfield Daily News*, January 4, 1932.

32. Ibid., January 7, 1932.

33. Ibid., January 4, 1932.

34. Ibid., January 4, 1932.

35. *Springfield Press*, January 4, 1932.

36. Records, clerk of County Court of Geeene County (Missouri), January 12, 1932, pp. 11, 37, 43, 88, 92.

37. *Houston Chronicle*, January 3, 1932.

38. *Houston Post-Dispatch*, January 3, 1932.

39. *Springfield Leader*, January 4, 1932.

40. *Springfield Daily News*, January 5, 1932.

41. Ibid.; *Springfield Press*, January 6, 1932.

42. *Springfield Leader*, January 5, 1932; *Springfield Daily News*, January 6, 1932.

43. Ibid., January 5, 1932; *Springfield Press*, January 7, 1932; *Springfield Leader*, January 7, 1932.

44. *Springfield Leader*, January 5, 1932.

45. Ibid.

46. Ibid., January 3, 1932; *Springfield Daily News*, January 4, 1932.

47. Ibid., January 5, 1932; *Springfield Leader*, January 5, 1932; *St. Louis Post-Dispatch*, January 6, 1932.

48. *Springfield Daily News*, January 4, 1932.

49. Files, circuit clerk of Greene County (Missouri), Record Book 29, p. 318, No. 97215C, *State* vs. *Oscar Young*, *State* vs. *Mrs. J. D. Young*.

CHAPTER 11: WORD GOES OUT: "FIND THE KILLERS"

1. *Springfield Leader*, January 3 and 4, 1932.

2. Ibid.; *Springfield Daily News,* January 5, 1932; *Springfield Leader,* January 5, 1932.

3. Personal recollection; *Springfield Leader,* January 6, 1932; Marie Haguewood Forrester, interview, May 30, 1981.

4. Dr. Lee Mirmow, Mills College, Oakland, California, personal communication, June 7, 1985.

5. *Springfield Leader,* January 4, 5, and 6, 1932.

6. Karen Pettijohn, secretary to registrar, Phillips University, Enid, Okla., private communication, October 23, 1985.

7. *Springfield Leader,* January 4, 1932; *Springfield Press,* January 5, 1932.

8. *Springfield Daily News,* January 4, 1932.

9. *Springfield Leader,* January 3, 1932.

10. *St. Louis Post-Dispatch,* January 4, 1932.

11. *Springfield Leader,* January 4, 1932; *Springfield News,* January 4, 1932.

12. *Springfield Press,* January 5, 1932, Extra.

13. *Houston Chronicle,* January 4, 1932.

14. Ibid.

15. Ibid.

16. *Houston Post-Dispatch,* January 5, 1932.

17. *Springfield Daily News,* January 5, 1932; *Houston Chronicle,* January 4, 1932.

18. *Springfield Daily News,* January 4, 1932.

19. Ibid.

20. Robert N. Hunter, chief engineer, Missouri Highway and Transportation Commission, private communication, December 30, 1985.

21. *Houston Post-Dispatch,* January 4 and 5, 1932; *Houston Chronicle,* January 4 and 5, 1932.

22. *St. Louis Post-Dispatch,* January 5, 1932; *Springfield Leader,* January 4, 1932; *Springfield Press,* January 5, 1932.

23. *Springfield Press,* January 5, 1932; *Houston Chronicle,* January 5, 1932.

24. *Houston Post-Dispatch,* January 6, 1932.

25. *Houston Chronicle,* January 4, 1932.

26. *Houston Post-Dispatch,* January 6, 1932; *Houston Chronicle,* January 5 and 6, 1932.

27. "Boy Delivering Chronicle Began Moves that Ended in Death of Slayers," *Houston Chronicle,* January 6, 1932.

28. Ibid.

29. Ibid. and *Houston Post-Dispatch,* January 6, 1932.

CHAPTER 12: THE SECOND SHOOTOUT

1. Carol S. Vance, district attorney, Harris County, Texas, private communication, February 22, 1972.

2. Joseph A. Jachimczyk, M.D., J.D., private communication, February 2, 1972.

3. *Houston Chronicle,* January 5, 1932; *Houston Post-Dispatch,* January 6, 1921.

4. *Springfield Leader,* January 5, 1932.

5. *Houston Chronicle,* January 5, 1932.

6. Ibid.

7. *Houston Post-Dispatch,* January 6, 1931.

8. *Houston Chronicle,* January 5, 1932.

9. *Springfield Press,* January 6, 1932.

10. *Houston Chronicle,* January 5, 1932.

11. *Springfield Leader,* January 5, 1932.

12. Robert Frost, "Dear Looiss," June 30, 1919, *The Letters of Robert Frost to Louis Untermeyer* (New York: Holt, Rinehart & Winston, 1963), p. 87.

13. Ibid.; *Springfield Daily News,* January 5, 1932; *Springfield Leader,* January 6, 1932.

14. *Springfield Press,* January 5, 1932.

CHAPTER 13: THE SURVIVORS' TALES

1. Chief of Police Sam Robards, interview, May 1972.

2. Vinita Young, telephone interview, November 4, 1984.

3. *Startling Detective Adventures,* April 1932; *True,* July 1932.

4. John R. Woodside, "Young Brothers' Massacre," unpublished pamphlet, pp. 20, 21.

5. *Springfield Press,* January 5, 1932. McLaughlin, *Souvenir Review.*

6. *Official Manual, State of Missouri, 1943-44* (Jefferson City, 1944).

7. Frank Pike, interviews, July 29, 1970, November 13, 1971.

8. Mrs. Frank Pike, interview, March 12, 1985; private communication, March 31, 1983.

9. *State* vs. *Ben Bilyeu et al,* case no. 53, December 31, 1908, Christian County (Missouri).

10. *State* vs. *Ben, Frank, Harlan, Lenzie Bilyeu,* August 21, 1917, Christian County (Missouri).

11. *State* vs. *Ben Bilyeu,* July 23, 1913, Christian County (Missouri). These files were all supplied by the late Sam Appleby, magistrate judge, Ozark, Christian County (Missouri).

CHAPTER 14: AFTERMATH OF DISASTER

1. *Springfield Leader,* January 3, 1932.

2. Coroner's Record and Fee Book, vol. 5, pp. 170, 171, office of clerk of County Court, Greene County (Missouri).

3. *Springfield Press,* January 5, 1932.

4. Ibid.

5. *Springfield Leader,* January 4, 1932; *Springfield Press,* January 5, 1932.

6. *Springfield Daily News,* January 5, 1932; *Springfield Press,* January 5, 1932.

7. *Springfield Daily News,* January 5, 1932.

8. *Springfield Leader,* January 5, 1932; *Springfield Press,* January 5, 1932.

9. *Springfield Leader,* January 4 and 5, 1932; *Springfield Daily News,* January 5 and 6, 1932.

10. *Springfield Leader,* January 7, 1932.

11. Ibid., January 4, 1932; *Springfield Daily News,* January 4, 1932.

12. Ibid.

13. *Springfield Press,* January 5, 1932.

14. Ibid., January 7, 1932; *Springfield Daily News,* January 8 and 11, 1932.

15. *Springfield Leader,* January 10, 1932; *Springfield Daily News,* January 10, 1932.

16. *Sunday News & Leader,* January 10, 1932.

17. *Springfield Leader,* January 6, 1932.

18. Ibid., quotes with datelines from *St. Louis Post-Dispatch, Joplin Globe, Carthage Press, St. Louis Star, Aurora Advertiser,* and *St. Joseph News-Press.*

19. *Springfield Leader,* January 6, 1932; *Springfield Daily News,* January 7, 1932.

20. Ibid.

21. *Springfield Leader,* January 13 and 14, 1932.

22. Ibid., January 7 and 8, 1932; *Springfield Daily News,* January 8, 1932.

23. *Springfield Daily News,* January 8, 1932; *St. Louis Post-Dispatch,* January 9, 1932.

24. *Springfield Leader,* January 13, 1932; *Springfield Daily News,* January 6, 1932.

25. Ibid.

26. *Springfield Leader,* January 5, 1932; *Springfield Daily News,* January 6, 1932.

27. *Springfield Leader,* January 3, 5, and 8, 1932; *Springfield Daily News,* January 4, 5, and 8, 1932; *Springfield Press,* January 5 and 6, 1932.

28. *Springfield Leader,* January 6, 1932; *Springfield Daily News,* January 7, 1932.

29. *Springfield Press,* January 6, 1932; *Springfield Leader,* January 10, 1932.

30. John R. Woodside, "Young Brothers' Massacre," unpublished pamphlet, p. 72.

31. Ray Oliver, interviews, November 11, 1970, March 18, 1985.

32. *Springfield Daily News,* January 4 and 5, 1932; *Springfield Leader,* January 6, 1932.

33. County Court Record, Greene County (Missouri), January 4, 1932, pp. 569–71.

34. *Houston Post-Dispatch,* January 8, 1932.

35. *Houston Chronicle,* January 6, 1932.

36. Boyd Armstrong, University of Houston, private communication, August 20, 1985.

37. *Houston Chronicle,* January 7, 1932.

38. *Springfield Press,* January 6 and 7, 1932.

39. *Houston Chronicle,* January 8 and 9, 1932; *Houston Post-Dispatch,* January 8, 1932.

40. Files, case no. 5430, Southern District Texas, Houston, March 1932, *U.S.* vs. *Paul Young and Mrs. J. B. Young, alias Willie Young.* File no. 4044,

U.S. District Court of Missouri, *U.S.* vs. *Paul Young, Mrs. J. B. Young, alias Willie Young,* March 8, 1932.

41. Carl F. Zarter, U.S. Penitentiary, Leavenworth, Kansas, private communication, September 30, 1966.

42. Files, U.S. District Court, Oklahoma, *U.S.* vs. *James Paul Young,* July 7, 1935, and docket sheet, September 21, 1935.

43. U.S. Department of Justice, Federal Bureau of Investigation, file no. 49.

44. *Springfield Press,* January 5, 1932.

45. John R. Woodside, private communication, September 25, 1970.

46. James C. Roberts, head, Reference Section, U.S. Copyright Office, three letters with circulars R4, R15, R15a, R15b, R22, undated (confirming telephone report of June 26, 1979).

47. *Springfield Leader,* January 17, 1942.

48. *Chicago Herald-American,* July 30, 1944.

49. *Bias,* December 26, 1951.

50. *Springfield Sunday News & Leader,* January 9, 1972.

51. *Springfield News & Leader,* January 3, 1972.

52. Frost, *Letters to Louis Untermeyer,* p. 196.

53. *Springfield News & Leader,* January 3, 1972.

EPILOGUE

1. *Springfield News-Leader,* April 13, 1986.

2. *Kansas City Times,* May 12, 1986.

3. *Time Magazine,* April 21, 1986.

4. *Parade Magazine,* September 28, 1986; *Jefferson City News & Tribune,* April 13, 1986; *Jefferson City Daily News,* April 14, 1986; *Springfield News-Leader,* April 13, 1986.